This book is dedicated to my beloved Ilan and Mira Dubler-Furman, and any siblings they have by now or in the future.

ALPHA BOOKS

Published by the Penguin Group

Penguin Group (USA) Inc., 375 Hudson Street, New York, New York 10014, USA

Penguin Group (Canada), 90 Eglinton Avenue East, Suite 700, Toronto, Ontario M4P 2Y3, Canada (a division of Pearson Penguin Canada Inc.)

Penguin Books Ltd., 80 Strand, London WC2R 0RL, England

Penguin Ireland, 25 St. Stephen's Green, Dublin 2, Ireland (a division of Penguin Books Ltd.)

Penguin Group (Australia), 250 Camberwell Road, Camberwell, Victoria 3124, Australia (a division of Pearson Australia Group Pty. Ltd.)

Penguin Books India Pvt. Ltd., 11 Community Centre, Panchsheel Park, New Delhi—110 017, India

Penguin Group (NZ), 67 Apollo Drive, Rosedale, North Shore, Auckland 1311, New Zealand (a division of Pearson New Zealand Ltd.)

Penguin Books (South Africa) (Pty.) Ltd., 24 Sturdee Avenue, Rosebank, Johannesburg 2196, South Africa

Penguin Books Ltd., Registered Offices: 80 Strand, London WC2R 0RL, England

Copyright © 2008 by Ellen Brown

International Standard Book Number: 978-1-59257-699-9
Library of Congress Catalog Card Number: 2007935859

10 09 08   8 7 6 5 4 3 2 1

Interpretation of the printing code: The rightmost number of the first series of numbers is the year of the book's printing; the rightmost number of the second series of numbers is the number of the book's printing. For example, a printing code of 08-1 shows that the first printing occurred in 2008.

Printed in the United States of America

Note: This publication contains the opinions and ideas of its author. It is intended to provide helpful and informative material on the subject matter covered. It is sold with the understanding that the author and publisher are not engaged in rendering professional services in the book. If the reader requires personal assistance or advice, a competent professional should be consulted.

The author and publisher specifically disclaim any responsibility for any liability, loss, or risk, personal or otherwise, which is incurred as a consequence, directly or indirectly, of the use and application of any of the contents of this book.

Most Alpha books are available at special quantity discounts for bulk purchases for sales promotions, premiums, fund-raising, or educational use. Special books, or book excerpts, can also be created to fit specific needs.

For details, write: Special Markets, Alpha Books, 375 Hudson Street, New York, NY 10014.

Publisher: *Marie Butler-Knight*
Editorial Director: *Mike Sanders*
Managing Editor: *Billy Fields*
Acquisitions Editor: *Michele Wells*
Senior Development Editor: *Christy Wagner*

Production Editor: *Kayla Dugger*
Copy Editor: *Tricia Liebig*
Book and Cover Designer: *Kurt Owens*
Layout: *Ayanna Lacey*
Proofreader: *Mary Hunt*

Introduction

No cliché has ever been as true as "necessity is the mother of invention." Imagine standing in the kitchen at midnight, ready to add brown sugar to your cookie dough … only to discover that the box is empty! That's not really a problem, as long as you have granulated sugar and molasses in the pantry. Or maybe your supermarket only has rock-hard mangoes, and you want to make a mango dessert for dinner. You're all set if you can find a good-looking papaya in the produce department.

Cooking isn't brain surgery, and recipes are very tolerant to changes in foodstuffs—you might even find that you like the results even better when made with the substitution! Baking is both an art and a science, but general cooking is open to endless variations, all of which can lead to successful results.

This book has been more than 30 years in the making, and I'm thrilled to be sharing with you the numerous tidbits I've learned in the kitchen and at the supermarket during the past decades. I've consulted myriad sources as I compiled the entries you'll find here, but many times it was to affirm substitution decisions I've been making successfully for years based on a combination of instinct and experience.

When I began cooking seriously in the early 1970s, I was a budding journalist at *The Cincinnati Enquirer*. At that time, you couldn't find a fresh snow pea in the city, let alone a complex herb blend like *herbes de Provence*. So I began to experiment and discovered that a julienne of green beans gave my Chinese stir-fries the same crunch and color as snow peas, and that by blending about a dozen herbs I could replicate the sunny flavors of the Provençale mixture.

Some of my experimentation springs from travel to parts of the world where cuisines are based on ingredients we can't find here. Professional cooks develop palate memory in the same way music critics develop aural memory; we compare and contrast one experience with another. I would keep the memory of a flavor, color, or texture with me when I returned home and then replicate a dish using what I could find locally.

There are numerous ways in which this book will make your life in the kitchen easier and more pleasant. Let's say you're midway through a recipe and realize that you're out of a key ingredient. No problem. Just flip to the alphabetical entry for what you're out of and you'll find an alternative or instructions on how to create one from foods you do have on hand.

I've noted the salient features of each ingredient to set up a standard from which the substitution is made. For example, because what defines mahi mahi is not only its dense, firm, off-white flesh but also its sweet flavor, I've looked at other aquatic species carefully before suggesting swordfish or halibut as the best "meaty" fish alternatives.

At other times, you might have perishable ingredients on hand and want to use them up. You can use this book as a check to ensure that the substitution you're about to make will work.

How to Use This Book

I've listed literally thousands of foods in the following pages, but not all have an individual listing. Many foods fall into families, such as dried pasta shapes or cheeses. I give these families in-depth treatment all together, and you'll see a cornucopia of substitutions in easy-to-follow tables. This is especially important for groups such as various wines specified in recipes. There's no reason to buy a Pinot Noir when any one of two dozen red wines will do, not to mention just a generic red table wine! So in the listings you'll find this:

> **Pinot Noir** (*pee-noh nwahr*)   *See* wine, red.

Or:

> **fontina** (*fon-TEE-nah*)   *See* cheese.

And to help you sound like a kitchen pro at your next party, I include pronunciations for many of the listings throughout. They are given in parentheses directly after the main listing.

Following the A to Z dictionary, you'll find three appendixes to further help make life easier. From tips on improvising kitchen equipment to metric conversions to yield and volume comparisons, you'll find a wealth of information at the back of the book.

Extras

Throughout the A to Z section, you'll find boxes that give you extra information—helpful for building knowledge of ingredients.

Toque Tips

You don't have to wear a tall white chef's hat (called a *toque*) to learn the tricks of this trade! Toque Tips boxes are full of cooking tips. Most are specific to the entry they accompany; others boost your general cooking skills or give you ideas for food presentation.

Food Foibles

It's always a good idea to be alerted to potential problems in advance. Food Foibles boxes provide warnings on ingredient selection or tip you off to storage or preparation problems.

Sub-Text

Cooking has a language all its own, and some of the terms can be intimidating if you don't know what they mean. Look to these boxes for definitions.

Acknowledgments

Writing a book is a solitary endeavor, but its publication is always a team effort. My thanks go to ...

Michele Wells of Alpha Books for needing a substitute for brown sugar, which spawned this idea. Ed Claflin, my agent, for his constant support and great humor. Christy Wagner, Tricia Liebig, and Linda Bilderback for their eagle-eyed editing. My many friends who willingly donated ideas from their cooking experiences, including Suzanne Cavedon, Janet Morell, Nancy Dubler, Nick Brown, and Kenn Speiser. Tigger-Cat Brown and Patches-Kitten Brown, for many hours of furry, purring support.

Special Thanks to the Technical Reviewer

The Complete Idiot's Guide to Cooking Substitutions was reviewed by an expert who double-checked the accuracy of what you'll learn here, to help us ensure that this book gives you everything you need to know about making great substitutions while you're cooking. Special thanks are extended to Leslie Bilderback.

Trademarks

All terms mentioned in this book that are known to be or are suspected of being trademarks or service marks have been appropriately capitalized. Alpha Books and Penguin Group (USA) Inc. cannot attest to the accuracy of this information. Use of a term in this book should not be regarded as affecting the validity of any trademark or service mark.

abalone   The flesh of this prized Pacific Coast mollusk is delicate in flavor. Clam and conch have a similar flavor and texture.

achiote seed   *See* annatto seed.

acidulated water   This really isn't an ingredient; it's a method of preventing foods like apples and artichokes from browning. It's frequently mentioned in recipes as if you should have a jar on the shelf. To substitute, add 3 tablespoons lemon juice or 2 tablespoons white vinegar to 1 quart water. Or crush 2 (500 mg) vitamin C tablets to a powder, and mix with 1 quart water.

acorn squash   This deep green squash with deep ridges has bright orange flesh and an innately sweet flavor. Any winter squash can be used interchangeably, especially butternut, Hubbard, or turban. Or substitute canned pumpkin; the texture is creamer but the flavor is similar.

adobo sauce (*ah-DOH-bo*)   This Mexican sauce is made from ground chilies, vinegar, and herbs. Hot red pepper sauce is the best alternative.

advocaat (*ad-voh-CAHT*)   *See* liqueur.

adzuki bean (*ad-ZOO-key*)   *See* beans, dried.

agar, agar-agar   This flavorless seaweed is used as a setting agent for cold foods. It's also called Japanese gelatin in some stores and is sold as powder. It only takes 1 teaspoon to set 1 cup liquid.

　　1 tsp. agar = 1³/₄ tsp. granular gelatin

agnolotti (*anyo-LOT-eeh*)   *See* pasta, stuffed.

ahi (*ah-he*)   *See* tuna.

aku (*ah-coo*)   *See* tuna.

Albariño (*ahl-bar-EEN-yo*)   *See* wine, white.

ale   *See* beer.

alfalfa sprouts   These germinated seeds are the thinnest and lightest of the commercially available sprouts. Sunflower sprouts are the closest, and mung bean sprouts are the most widely available.

all-purpose flour   *See* flour.

allspice   This characteristic flavor in ketchup was so named because its aroma is reminiscent of a blend of cloves, cinnamon, and nutmeg; its flavor is pungent like pepper.

> *1 tsp. ground allspice = ¹/₄ tsp. ground cloves + ¹/₄ tsp. ground nutmeg + ¹/₄ tsp. ground cinnamon + ¹/₄ tsp. freshly ground black pepper*

almond   Almonds fall on the mildly flavored side of the spectrum, so both macadamia nuts and pine nuts are good substitutes.

almond butter   While commercial almond butter is becoming more common, especially at health food stores, cashew butter is the best substitute. Peanut butter is too strong in flavor.

almond extract   This very concentrated and pungent extract is used most frequently in desserts and baked goods to deliver a decidedly almond flavor. Use 1 tablespoon almond liqueur for each ¼ teaspoon pure almond extract and adjust the liquid in the recipe accordingly.

almond paste   *See* marzipan.

amaretti (*ah-mar-ETT-e*)   These crisp Italian meringue cookies are made with bitter almond paste, and they're usually crushed and added to desserts. Almond biscotti are the best substitute, with ¼ teaspoon pure almond extract added per 1 cup crumbs, or use any light meringue cookie and add ½ teaspoon almond extract per 1 cup crumbs.

amaretto (*ah-mar-ETT-oh*)   *See* liqueur, nut.

Amarone (*ah-mar-OH-nay*)   *See* wine, red.

American cheese   *See* cheese.

Anaheim chili   *See* chilies, fresh.

anasazi beans (*ah-nah-SAH-zee*)   *See* beans, dried.

ancho chili (*AHN-cho*)   *See* chilies, dried.

anchovy   It's becoming more common to find mild-tasting white anchovies, but pungent, salty, and fishy-tasting fillets packed in olive oil are readily available (the red color is due to the curing process). Asian fish sauce (*nam pla*) is anchovy-based. Use 2 tablespoons fish sauce for each 1 anchovy fillet. Or soak salt cod for 15 minutes in boiling water and then purée. Use 1 tablespoon purée for each anchovy fillet.

anchovy paste   Anchovies are usually chopped or mashed to spread their fishy flavor, but the paste is already in that state.

1 TB. anchovy paste = 5 anchovy fillets, puréed

> **Toque Tips**
>
> To easily mash anchovies to a smooth paste, put the fillets through a garlic press.

andouille sausage (*ahn-DOO-ee*)   This spicy smoked sausage from Louisiana is a staple of Cajun cooking. Polish kielbasa or other smoked sausages are good substitutes, but you'll want to add hot red pepper sauce or cayenne to replicate the heat.

anelli (*ah-NEH-lee*)   *See* pasta, dried.

angel food cake   This popular cake is so named for its light, airy texture. Few cakes are made without egg yolks, but sponge cake is the one closest in texture to angel food cake.

anglerfish   *See* monkfish.

anise   *See* fennel.

anise seed   These tiny gray seeds, always used whole, are from an herb in the parsley family. They deliver a strong licorice flavor.

1 tsp. anise seed = 1 TB. anise-flavored liqueur such as Pernod or ouzo; subtract 1 TB. from the liquid specified in a recipe

Anjou pear (*ahn-jhu*)   *See* pear.

annatto seed (*ahn-YAH-toh*)   These seeds removed from furry pods of Caribbean and Latin American trees give dishes a vivid red color. Either crush them before using or heat them in oil to transfer their color.

1 tsp. ground annatto = 1 TB. sweet paprika

antelope   *See* game meat.

apéritif (*ah-pear-uh-teev*)   *See* wine, apéritif.

apple   The more than 300 varieties of apples grown in North America present a wide range of apple flavors as well as textures. All are crisp and juicy when you bite into them raw, and they develop a mellower flavor when cooked. About 2½ to 3 pounds of apples make a 9-inch pie.

Here are the major varieties found in North American markets:

Cortland   This medium to large all-purpose apple is crisp, juicy, and has both sweet and tart flavors. It is a rich red color, at times striped with green. The flesh is very white and resists browning, so it's well suited for salads and fruit displays.

Empire   This beautiful, large, juicy red apple has a sweet, almost spicy flavor. It's wonderful baked as well as eaten fresh.

Fuji   Introduced to the United States from Japan in the 1980s, this large super-sweet apple has Red Delicious as one parent. It's good for baking and salads.

Golden Delicious   This round, rich-yellow apple offers a spectrum of flavors, from slightly tart to mellow and sweet. The skin color ranges from light green to pale or creamy yellow, depending upon the maturity. The more yellow the skin, the sweeter the apple.

Granny Smith   This tart, all-purpose apple is gaining popularity for its tart flavor, its firm flesh that retains texture when cooked, and its uniformity. The Granny's flavor tends to vary from mild to very tart, and on occasion, the texture may be a bit on the dry side. Look for firm and brightly colored apples.

Jonathan   A medium-size red apple with a yellow blush, it has firm, crisp, juicy flesh and is particularly well suited for pies and baking whole because it holds its shape very well. It's an excellent all-purpose apple.

A

McIntosh   This medium-size red-on-green apple has a crisp, sweet, aromatic flesh. It's excellent for eating and making applesauce, but it doesn't hold its shape well for pies or baking whole.

Red Delicious   Look for smooth bright skins, richly colored crimson, sometimes streaked with yellow or sometimes a yellow cheek. This apple is easily recognized by the knobs at the base.

Winesap   This bright, all-purpose apple with an old-fashioned tangy taste has crisp, crunchy, juicy flesh with a sweet-tart flavor. Look for apples with smooth, glossy, bright red skin with hints of purple.

Toque Tips

Here's a quick and easy way to slice apples: after you've peeled the apple, start shaving off slices from the outside with a paring knife, turning the apple in quarter turns. Continue slicing until you reach the core and then discard the core.

If the apple specified in a recipe isn't available, use one with the same rating shown in the following table.

Apple Varieties and Uses

Variety	Eating	Baking Whole	Pie
Cortland	good	good	fair
Empire	excellent	fair	fair
Fuji	good	excellent	poor
Golden Delicious	good	good	excellent
Granny Smith	fair	good	excellent
Jonathan	excellent	excellent	excellent
McIntosh	good	poor	fair
Newton Pippin	good	excellent	excellent
Red Delicious	good	fair	fair
Winesap	excellent	good	good

apple cider, apple juice   These two can be used interchangeably, although freshly pressed apple cider delivers far more apple flavor. In a pinch, white grape juice is the best substitute.

apple pie spice   This blending of aromatic spices includes all those listed separately in most recipes, with cinnamon as the dominant one. You can always use cinnamon; pumpkin pie spice is a similar mix that also includes ginger.

> *1 TB. apple pie spice = $1^1/_2$ tsp. ground cinnamon + 1 tsp. ground nutmeg + $^1/_4$ tsp. ground cloves + $^1/_4$ tsp. ground allspice*

applejack   *See* brandy.

applesauce   This purée of cooked apples, sometimes sweetened and sometimes natural, can be either chunky or smooth. If you want a smooth sauce, substitute strained apple baby food. Or make it yourself— it's so easy you might never buy a jar again!

Yield: $1^1/_2$ cups

4 McIntosh apples
$^1/_3$ cup dry white wine or water
2 TB. dark rum (optional)

2 TB. firmly packed dark brown sugar
2 TB. granulated sugar
$^1/_4$ tsp. ground cinnamon (optional)

Peel, quarter, and core apples. Cut apples into thin slices. Place apples in a saucepan and add wine, rum (if using), brown sugar, granulated sugar, and cinnamon (if using). Bring to a boil over medium-high heat. Reduce heat to low, and cook apples, stirring occasionally, for 20 to 30 minutes or until soft. For chunky applesauce, mash apples with a potato masher. For smooth applesauce, transfer apples to a food processor fitted with a steel blade and purée until smooth. Applesauce will keep up to a week refrigerated and tightly covered.

---

apricots, dried   It takes about 6 pounds fresh apricots to make 1 pound dried, so it's not surprising that the flavor of dried apricots is so intense. Dried mango or peaches are the best substitutes both for flavor and color. Also look for "fruit leathers." These are purées of dried fruit spread on cellophane, and apricot is one of the most common flavors.

apricots, fresh These tiny, tangy fruits have a unique and intense flavor, but there are ways to compensate if you don't have fresh apricots. Use ripe peaches or nectarines instead of apricots and add one part rehydrated dried apricot purée to four parts peaches to replicate the flavor.

aquavit (*AKWA-veet*) This Swedish liqueur is distilled from potatoes and flavored with caraway seeds. The best way to replicate its flavor is to crush caraway seeds and add them to vodka. Allow the mixture to infuse for at least 2 days and then drain it.

arborio rice (*ahr-BOAR-e-yoh*) *See* rice.

Ardennes ham (*ahr-denz*) *See* ham.

Armagnac (*arm-an-yak*) *See* brandy.

arrowroot This powder made from the dried roots of a tropical tuber is used as a thickening agent. When adding it to a simmering liquid, always mix it with water first to prevent clumping.

> *1 tsp. arrowroot = 2 tsp. cornstarch + 2 tsp. potato starch; or 1 TB. all-purpose flour*

artichoke There really is no vegetable close to an artichoke in flavor, although the color of cooked eggplant is similar.

> *1 (10-oz.) pkg. frozen artichoke hearts = 4 fresh artichoke bottoms*

Toque Tips

Not sure how to eat an artichoke? Begin with the outer leaves. Hold the leaf from the top, and remove it from artichoke. Dip the bottom part into the sauce. Scrape off the tender flesh between your teeth. When you come to the "cone" (the tender central leaves), pull the cone from the artichoke; most of these leaves are edible. Underneath the cone is a cluster of small leaves under which is a hairy growth, the choke, that covers the deliciously edible bottom of the artichoke. Scrape out and discard the choke, and cut the bottom into bite-size pieces.

arugula (*ah-RU-go-lah*)   *See* lettuce.

asadero (*ah-sah-DARE-oh*)   *See* cheese.

asiago (*ah-SAH-gee-oh*)   *See* cheese.

Asian pear   This fruit has the flavor of a pear with the texture of an apple, and they're almost round in shape with a yellow-green skin. Apples are the best stand-in; add some pear nectar to the recipe for flavor.

asparagus   You'll find expensive white and rare purple asparagus on the market, but the vast majority of this grassy-tasting vegetable takes the form of green stalks that vary from thinner than pencils to about ½ inch in diameter. Although no vegetable has the same flavor, you can sub either broccoli or green beans when cooking.

Asti Spumante   *See* wine, sparkling.

Atlantic cod   *See* cod.

Atlantic croaker   *See* drum.

avocado   There's really no substitute for the buttery-rich pale green fruit of this fruit we eat as a vegetable, but to reduce calories, you can substitute cooked and mashed zucchini or yellow squash.

Toque Tips

If you find that an avocado is not ripe when you cut it open, coat the cut edges with mayonnaise, push it back together, and allow it to continue ripening at room temperature. Wipe off the mayonnaise when you're ready to eat.

bacon What we call bacon is the pig's fatty chest meat that's brined and then smoked and must be cooked before eating. As a seasoning, salt pork is the best substitute, but for eating, try smoked sausage or ham.

There are other related foods:

fatback This literally is fat from the pig's back, and it's typically used to add fat and moisture to foods. Substitute salt pork—it's the same cut— but simmer it for 10 minutes first to extract some of the salt.

pancetta This thick Italian bacon is sold in cylindrical form. It's salty but doesn't have the smoky taste of American bacon. It's not eaten by itself; it's used to flavor soups and sauces. American bacon is the best substitute; the fatty rinds of Italian prosciutto can also be used.

salt pork This is the back fat of the pork that's been dry-salted. Although it does contain some meat, it's used only as a seasoning. Fatback is the best substitute, but use some additional salt in the dish.

Toque Tips

Take a tip from food producers; precook your bacon. Cook it until it's about 80 percent crisp and then drain and freeze it. When you're craving a BLT, just "nuke" a few slices. I do a few pounds at a time, and it lasts for a few months frozen.

bacon, Canadian Although we call it bacon and it's cured, this lean cut is actually the eye of the pig's loin. Smoked ham or boneless smoked pork chops are similar in flavor and almost identical in appearance.

baking chocolate   *See* chocolate.

baking mix   Find a recipe that calls for a premixed product like Bisquick? No problem; you can make it yourself.

Yield: 2½ cups

1 cup all-purpose flour
1 cup cake flour
½ cup powdered milk
1 TB. baking powder

½ tsp. salt
6 TB. unsalted butter, cut into small bits

Combine all-purpose flour, cake flour, powdered milk, baking powder, and salt in a mixing bowl. Cut in butter using a pastry blender, two knives, or your fingertips until mixture resembles coarse meal. Store refrigerated in an airtight container for up to 3 weeks.

Variation: If you're making biscuits, use powdered buttermilk in place of the powdered milk.

---

baking powder   The baking powder we use most often is double-acting, which means two different compounds work as leavening agents during different parts of the baking cycle.

   1 tsp. baking powder = ½ tsp. baking soda + ½ tsp. cream of tartar

baking soda   Also called bicarbonate of soda, this leavening agent must be combined with an acidic ingredient such as buttermilk to create carbon dioxide bubbles. It is twice as strong as baking powder, so use 1 teaspoon baking powder for each ½ teaspoon baking soda.

balsamic vinegar   *See* vinegar.

bamboo shoot   These are actually young and tender roots of an edible bamboo plant. Finding them fresh is nearly impossible; they're always canned and sliced in the Asian section of supermarkets. Jicama slices, cooked until just tender, have the same bland flavor.

banana   This fruit from the tropics is almost universally available, but ripe plantains are the only food even close to them in flavor and texture. If you're using bananas in baking, try puréed baby food.

B

Toque Tips

Have some bananas getting past their prime? Throw them into the freezer, peels and all. The next time you want to make banana bread, thaw them and they're ready to mash. Or, if you're a smoothie fan, freeze them in slices and then blend away!

banana, green   You'll find unripe bananas listed in Caribbean recipes; plantains are the best alternative.

Banyuls (*ban-youls*)   *See* wine, dessert.

Barbaresco (*bahr-bah-RES-koh*)   *See* wine, red.

barbecue sauce   Barbecue sauce is used either to baste food while it grills or as a condiment. To substitute, mix 1 cup ketchup with ¼ cup firmly packed dark brown sugar and ½ cup cider vinegar.

Barbera (*bahr-BEAR-ah*)   *See* wine, red.

Bardolino (*bar-do-LEAN-oh*)   *See* wine, red.

barley   This tiny, mild-flavored grain with a chewy texture is most often used in soups, but it's also good in salads. Short-grain Japanese rice has the same visual effect, as do tiny pastas like pastina and orzo. Within the grain family, bulgur is the best alternative. However, the cooking times will be far faster with these alternatives.

Barolo (*bah-ROH-low*)   *See* wine, red.

Barsac (*bahr-sack*)   *See* wine, dessert.

Bartlett pear   *See* pear.

basil   There are more than 150 varieties of this aromatic herb of the mint family that has a rich, spicy, and mildly peppery flavor. The popularity of basil spans the globe; it's used in Italian and other Mediterranean cuisines and also in Thai cooking. Any variety of basil can be substituted for each other, and if all else fails, use 1 tablespoon dried basil and ½ cup chopped fresh Italian parsley for each ½ cup basil in a recipe.

1 TB. chopped fresh basil = 1 tsp. dried basil or 1 tsp. Italian seasoning

Basil at a Glance

Basil	Description
Common (Genovese)	Sweet-tasting and aromatic with large leaves
Greek	Sweet-tasting and aromatic with very small leaves
Lemon	Hints of lemon, licorice, and cinnamon; from Asia
Opal	Sweet-tasting and aromatic with bright purple leaves
Thai	Spicy flavor; from Asia

basmati rice (*baas-MAH-tee*)   *See* rice.

bay leaf   Also called bay laurel and sweet bay, these aromatic leaves should always be removed before a dish is served because they are extremely bitter if eaten. You can often find them fresh, although a cache of dried leaves always comes in handy.

1 fresh bay leaf = 2 dried bay leaves

Bayonne ham (*bay-yohn*)   *See* ham.

bean curd   *See* tofu.

bean sprout   It used to be that the only fresh bean sprouts sold were the thick mung bean sprouts used in Asian cooking, but that's no longer the case. Delicate alfalfa sprouts as well as sprouts from radishes, lentils, soybeans, and wheat berries are now common. Any sprout can be substituted for another, but only mung bean sprouts should be cooked; the others are far too delicate and will fall apart. Julienne strips of bok choy, Napa cabbage, or celery can stand in for bean sprouts in a cooked dish.

Food Foibles

Bean sprouts are one of the most perishable vegetables and should be used within 2 days. If you smell any off odor or if the sprouts feel slimy, throw them out. To preserve bean sprouts, refrigerate them in cold water, and change the water daily.

bean thread noodles *See* cellophane noodles.

beans, dried Every cuisine has a role for the legume, and a few bags in the pantry always come in handy. With the exception of quick-cooking lentils and split peas, all dried beans should be soaked to speed up the cooking time. Soak beans at room temperature for a minimum of 6 hours, or bring them to a boil and then soak them, covered, for 1 hour. In general, 1 pound dried beans makes 5 or 6 cups cooked beans.

Size, flavor, and cooking time are the criteria for deciding what bean can be substituted for another. Use the following table to find an appropriate replacement.

Dried Beans at a Glance

Bean	Description	Substitutions
adzuki	small, round, orange, and sweet	red kidney
anasazi	red and white striped, sweet	pinto
black (also called turtle)	small black with white flesh	pinto, red kidney
black-eyed peas	cream with dot, sweet	navy
cannellini	white oval shape	navy or Great Northern
cranberry (also called shell beans)	large, white with red streaks	anasazi, pinto
fava	very large, light brown	large lima
flageolet	small light green or white	navy
garbanzo	small, round, and beige with a nutty flavor	Great Northern, cannellini
Great Northern	medium, white, and oval	cannellini, navy
kidney	oval, medium, red	pinto

continues

Dried Beans at a Glance   (continued)

Bean	Description	Substitutions
lima		
small	round, thin, sweet	navy, cannellini
large	very large, white	fava, small lima
navy	small, oval, white	cannellini, flageolet
pinto	medium oval, beige with pink	kidney

Food Foibles

Don't add salt to the water in which beans are soaking or cooking because it will toughen the skins and prevent water absorption. Any acid such as tomato or wine will also cause the beans to take longer to soften.

Beaujolais (*bow-zhuh-lay*)   *See* wine, red.

béchamel (*bech-ah-mell*)   *See* white sauce.

beef   The number of names given to parts of the common cow are dizzying, and some are not even consistent in different parts of the country. The good news is, with rare exceptions—a standing rib roast is a standing rib roast—almost any cut specified in a recipe has at least one stand-in.

Beef is graded by the U.S. Department of Agriculture as *prime, choice,* or *standard.* Prime is usually reserved for restaurants, and the other two are what we buy in supermarkets. The category is determined by the age, color, texture, and *marbling* of the beef. Prime beef is the most marbled and contains the most fat. Look for deep red, moist meat generously marbled with white fat because yellow fat betrays old age. Beef is purple after cutting, but the meat quickly "blooms" to bright red with exposure to air. Well-aged beef is dark and dry. To avoid paying for waste, be sure to have your meat thoroughly trimmed by a butcher.

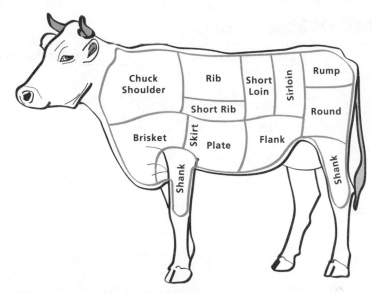

The various cuts of meat from a cow.

Sub-Text

Marbling is the fat patterns that swirl through some cuts of meat. Although you don't want marbling in lean cuts of meat like tenderloin, the fat, which leaches out of the meat during slow cooking, is desirable for less-expensive cuts because it punctuates the strong muscle fibers and makes the food tender after cooking.

Cuts for braising are less expensive than those for grilling or roasting. Many times a recipe gives you a generic term like "pot roast." Technically, that isn't a cut of beef; it's a description of the cooking method that can be used on any number of inexpensive large cuts. Consult the following table and always feel free to choose a cut on sale as long as it fulfills the same function.

"Stewing beef" is another generic category. It's usually cut from the chuck, and you pay a premium price to buy it already cut up. Save some money and instead spend a few minutes cutting it yourself. In addition to saving money, there are many advantages to cutting meat yourself: you can trim off all visible fat, you can make the pieces a uniform size or the size specified in the recipe, and you can save the scraps for grinding into hamburger or making stock.

Beef at a Glance

Beef	Origin	Cooking Method(s)
Arm steak	chuck round	braise
Blade steak	chuck shoulder	braise
Bottom round	round	braise
Brisket	chuck	braise
Châteaubriand	tenderloin	roast, grill
Chuck roast	chuck	braise
Club steak	short loin	grill, sauté
Cube steak	top butt	grill, sauté
Delmonico steak	short loin	grill, sauté
Eye of round	round	braise
Filet mignon	tenderloin	grill, sauté
Flank steak	flank	grill, sauté
Flanken	rib plate	braise
London broil	flank	grill, sauté
Minute steak	top butt	grill, sauté
New York strip	top loin	grill, sauté
Porterhouse	short loin	grill, sauté
Pot roast	chuck, round, or rump	braise
Prime rib	rib	roast
Rib eye steak	rib	grill, sauté
Round steak	round	grill, braise, kebabs
Rump roast	rump	roast, braise, kebabs
Short ribs	rib plate	braise
Sirloin roast	loin	roast, grill

Beef	Origin	Cooking Method(s)
Sirloin steak	loin	grill, sauté
Sirloin tip	loin	grill, sauté, kebabs

Another quandary when cooking beef is when you change from boneless cuts to those with bones. Refer to the following table to determine how much you'll need.

Beef Per Person

Cut	With Bone	Without Bone
Pot roast	10 to 12 oz.	8 to 10 oz.
Short ribs	1 to 1½ lb.	8 to 10 oz.
Standing rib roast	1 rib per 2 people	n/a
Steak	12 to 14 oz.	6 to 8 oz.
Stewing beef	n/a	8 to 10 oz.

beef, ground   The ratio of meat to fat determines the cost of ground beef, and many packages are also labeled with the source of the beef (sirloin, chuck, and so on). The best burgers are made with ground chuck, a meat that's 80 percent lean. Ground chuck must come from the very well-marbled and flavorful chuck, and should you want a leaner burger, look for ground sirloin. Ground lamb can be substituted for ground beef and adds its distinctive flavor to a dish, or to trim the fat, use more ground turkey.

beer   What characterizes all members of the beer family—including ale, bock beer, lager, Pilsner, and stout—is the yeast used in fermentation so the mixture bubbles. Usually low in alcohol (most are between 4 and 10 percent), beer is brewed from malted barley and other cereal grains, and it can range in color from very pale to almost black. When cooking with beer, its innate bitterness becomes a flavor in the finished dish.

1 cup beer = 1 cup stock + ½ tsp. bitters (for cooking) or 1 cup club soda + ½ tsp. bitters (for batters)

Beerenauslese (*BAY-rhun-OWSH-lay-zeh*)   *See* wine, sweet.

beet greens   You get a bonus with beets because the leafy green tops can be sautéed or steamed. Swiss chard and spinach are substitutes for beet greens.

beets   Beets now come in a golden color as well as the traditional red, and both have the same sweet flavor. Although the red color can only be replicated by red cabbage, the same sweet flavor is possible by cooking a combination of carrots and parsnips, which will give you a golden color.

Bel Paese (*bell pie-YAY-zay*)   *See* cheese.

Belgian endive   *See* lettuce.

bell pepper   Versatile and mild-flavored, bell peppers are so named because of their shape. The seeds are the sign that they're related to tomatoes and eggplant; they're all members of the nightshade family. Green peppers are immature red peppers, and they're less expensive because they're not as perishable. Either Anaheim or poblano chilies are the best substitute for green bell peppers, although their flavors are slightly spicy; any of the colored peppers can be substituted for one another. If the pepper is to be roasted and peeled, any of the jarred, preroasted peppers are just as good—and save a lot of time.

belon oyster (*bell-on*)   *See* oyster.

beluga (*bell-OU-gah*)   *See* caviar.

Bénédictine   *See* liqueur.

Bermuda onion   *See* onion.

beurre manié (*burr man-yeh*)   Used as a thickening agent for sauces, soups, and stews, this compound is equal parts softened butter and all-purpose flour.

2 TB. beurre manié = 1 TB. cornstarch mixed with 2 TB. cold water

bibb lettuce   *See* lettuce.

bicarbonate of soda   *See* baking soda.

biscotti (*bis-KOTT-ee*)   These Italian cookies are so hard because they're baked twice. Eastern European Mandelbrot, Dutch rusk, or German zwieback are similar concepts.

bitters   The liquid used as an accent in drinks such as champagne cocktails and Manhattans is a distillation of herbs, roots, and other vegetal scraps—and it's *really* bitter. Worcestershire sauce has a similar flavor, or you can add some very strongly brewed black tea.

black bean   *See* beans, dried.

black bean, fermented   *See* fermented black bean.

Black Forest ham   *See* ham.

black pepper, black peppercorn   *See* peppercorn.

black sea bass   The flesh of this Atlantic fish is firm, white, and delicately flavored. Black sea bass is often served whole in Chinese restaurants because it holds together well fried or steamed. Grouper, red snapper, and ocean perch are the best substitutions.

black trumpet mushroom   *See* mushroom, wild.

blackberry   Marion berries, native to Northwest states such as Oregon and Washington, are the closest in taste, color, and size to blackberries. Black raspberries are also a good choice.

black-eyed pea   *See* beans, dried.

blackfin   *See* tuna.

blackstrap   *See* molasses.

blanc de blancs (*blahn duh blahngk*)   *See* wine, sparkling.

blended whiskey   *See* spirits.

bleu cheese   *See* cheese.

blini (*BLEE-knee*)   These tiny buckwheat pancakes are usually topped with caviar or smoked salmon. Try buttered toast made with thin slices of whole-wheat bread for about the same flavor.

blood orange   These tart oranges are distinguished by their bright, hot pink juice. Reduce regular orange juice by ⅓ to intensify its flavor and then add a few drops of red food coloring or grenadine for color.

blue crab   *See* crab.

Blue Point oyster   *See* oyster.

blueberry   Although they're slightly more tart, huckleberries can be used interchangeably with blueberries in any recipe. Or for serving fresh, black raspberries or blackberries are also a good choice.

bluefin   *See* tuna.

bluefish   The flavor of this fish from the North Atlantic is mild when very fresh; however, it becomes very strong within a day after being caught due to its high oil content. Mackerel is the only other fish that shares its flavor profile.

boar   *See* game meat.

bok choy   This Chinese cabbage grows in stalks similar to celery, with dark green, leafy tops on snowy white ribs. While stalks can be large, you can also find baby bok choy that are only about 6 inches long. Napa cabbage, celery, and green cabbage are the best substitutes for the ribs; Swiss chard and spinach are the best stand-ins for the leaves.

bologna   This precooked luncheon meat is named for the Italian city of Bologna, and mortadella (the authentic Italian sausage) has the same basic flavor with some cubes of fat added. If the bologna is to be cooked, substitute hot dogs or knockwurst.

bonita   *See* tuna.

Bosc pear   *See* pear.

Boston lettuce   *See* lettuce.

bouillon   *See* stock.

bouquet garni (*boo-kay gar-knee*)   This combination of herbs is used as a flavoring for soups, stocks, and stews in classic French cooking. Combine 1 or 2 bay leaves, 2 sprigs fresh parsley, 1 sprig fresh thyme, and 12 black peppercorns in a piece of cheesecloth or insert them into a metal tea infuser to make retrieving them easier.

bourbon   *See* spirits.

boursault (*boar-soh*)   *See* cheese.

boursin (*boar-san*)   *See* cheese.

boysenberry   This berry hybrid is a cross between raspberries, blackberries, and loganberries, although they look like large raspberries. Any combination of the component berries can be used.

brains   Calf's brains are considered the most delicate; however, brains from lambs, pigs, or larger beef can be used. Of the other organ meats, sweetbreads (the thymus gland of veal calves) are the best substitute.

brandy   This medium-brown, distilled after-dinner beverage is made from grapes unless otherwise noted, and because of its high alcohol content—it's usually between 40 to 60 percent alcohol—and intense flavor, a little goes a long way. Under the general classification of brandy, certain are region-specific; cognac and Armagnac are made in their respective regions of France. Italian grappa is generic and is made from fermented grape pulp, seeds, and stems, but the flavor is similar. Metaxa is a classic Greek brandy.

2 TB. brandy = 1 tsp. brandy extract + 5 tsp. water; 1 tsp. brandy extract + 5 tsp. vodka; or 2 TB. bourbon

brandy, fruit   In addition to grape brandies, many other fruits and their juices are distilled, and these brandies can range from clear and very tart to somewhat sweet. Calvados, from the Normandy region of France, is far more refined and tart than American applejack. Kirsch (also called kirschwasser) is the clear, tart cherry brandy used in classic cheese fondue. When finding a substitute for a fruit brandy, the best choice is to use brandy and then add the fruit flavor with dried fruit. If time permits, you can infuse the brandy with the chopped dried fruit, or else add the fruit to the recipe.

2 TB. fruit brandy = 2 TB. brandy + 2 TB. chopped dried fruit of the appropriate flavor

bratwurst (*BRAT-vurst*)   Weisswurst and bockwurst both have the same delicate flavor as these German pork and veal sausages.

Brazil nut   These huge nuts have a very delicate flavor, so either macadamia nuts or blanched almonds are the best nuts to substitute.

breadcrumbs   Used as a binder, as a coating, and as a topping, breadcrumbs are an essential part of every kitchen. You can also use equal amounts of cracker crumbs, rolled oats, cornmeal, or matzoh meal.

Breakfast cereals such as cornflakes or puffed rice cereal can be ground into crumbs, too. If you have rock-hard stale bread, you can make your own. Break stale bread into pieces no larger than ½ inch and place the cubes in a food processor fitted with a steel blade. Pulse on and off until the crumbs are ground finely. If your bread is fresh, preheat the oven to 375°F and bake the slices for 7 to 10 minutes per side or until dry and then proceed as directed for stale bread. *See also* panko.

breadcrumbs, Italian   These breadcrumbs have already been seasoned. To replicate the flavor, add ¼ cup freshly grated Parmesan cheese, 1 tablespoon Italian seasoning, and ½ teaspoon salt to each 1 cup plain breadcrumbs.

Brie (*bree*)   *See* cheese.

brill   Turbot, Dover sole, flounder, and cod are the best substitutes for this mild-flavored European fish.

Brillat-Savarin (*bre-yat sah-vear-ahn*)   *See* cheese.

brioche (*bree-osh*)   This classic French breakfast bread is loaded with butter and eggs. Challah is equally high in egg content, and croissants have a similar butter content but are crisper when baked.

brisket   *See* beef.

broad bean   *See* fava bean.

broccoli   If you're after broccoli's green color, use Brussels sprouts, green cauliflower, or broccoli rabe in place of broccoli; the broccoli rabe will be decidedly more bitter, though. If color doesn't matter, any cauliflower has a taste similar to broccoli. In creamed soups, try either asparagus or spinach.

Toque Tips

If you want to avoid the "broccoli smell" in the house when cooking, add a slice of bread to the water in the pot.

broccoli rabe (or **rapini**)   *See* greens.

broth   *See* stock.

brown rice *See* rice.

brown sauce This backbone of classic French cooking comes from hours of simmering, but by using prepared stock, you can shortcut the time. You can use packets of dehydrated brown sauce mix from the supermarket or make it yourself:

Yield: 1½ cups

2 (14.5-oz.) cans beef stock, preferably reduced sodium
1 medium onion, peeled and diced
1 carrot, scrubbed and sliced
1 celery rib, rinsed and sliced
4 sprigs fresh parsley
1 sprig fresh thyme or ½ tsp. dried

1 bay leaf
12 peppercorns
1 TB. cornstarch
2 TB. cold water
2 TB. unsalted butter, cut into bits
Freshly ground black pepper

Combine stock, onion, carrot, celery, parsley, thyme, bay leaf, and peppercorns in a saucepan. Bring to a boil over high heat, reduce the heat to medium, and boil for 15 minutes or until reduced by ⅔. Strain stock, pressing with the back of a spoon to extract as much liquid as possible. Discard solids, return stock to the saucepan, and bring stock back to a boil. In a small bowl or cup, mix cornstarch with water. Add mixture to stock, and simmer for 2 minutes or until bubbly and slightly thickened. Add butter and swirl pan until butter melts. Season with pepper. Sauce can be refrigerated for up to 4 days, tightly covered.

---

brown sugar *See* sugar.

Brunello di Montalcino (*broo-NEH-loh dee mohn-tahl-CHEE-noh*) *See* wine, red.

bruschetta (*brew-SKET-tah*) This has become a generic name for a slice of toast rubbed with garlic and olive oil, and you can make it from any loaf of unflavored white bread.

Brussels sprout   The fact that they resemble tiny heads of cabbage should be a tip-off for what you can use as a substitute. Try either green or Savoy cabbage, diced or sliced to the same size as a Brussels sprout.

Bûcheron (*booch-eran*)   *See* cheese.

buckwheat groats   Buckwheat, frequently sold under the name kasha, has a nutty flavor, and it's usually sold roasted. Brown rice, quinoa, and bulgur are the best substitutes, although the cooking time will be longer.

buffalo   *See* game meat.

buffalo mozzarella   *See* cheese.

bulgur (*BULL-ghr*)   These whole kernels of wheat have been washed, steamed, had the hull removed, and then cracked into various granulations. Bulgur is similar to cracked wheat, but is precooked so it has a deeper gold color and a toastier flavor. Buckwheat and quinoa are both good substitutes.

butter   Butter comes from churning cream, and modern appliances have made this a snap at home. Thoroughly chill a blender jar and add 1 cup light cream. Blend at high speed just until the cream coats the blades, about 15 seconds. Then add ½ cup ice water through the lid and blend at high speed until the butter rises to the surface. Drain and keep refrigerated. You can also use stick margarine as a substitute on a direct basis. *See also* fats and oils.

Food Foibles

Whipped butter is not a substitute for butter because the measurements are not the same. If you're using whipped butter for baking, remember it takes ¾ cup to equal ½ cup of stick butter.

butter, clarified   The purpose of clarifying butter is to remove the dairy solids at which point the liquid is pure fat with a much higher smoke point. Ghee, found in Indian grocery stores, is a form of clarified butter and a good replacement. Or you can make clarified butter yourself. Melt unsalted butter over low heat and then refrigerate the pan. Scoop off the hardened butter, and discard the milk solids at the bottom of the pan.

butter bean   *See* lima bean.

buttermilk   Technically, buttermilk was the liquid left after butter was churned, but today it's milk with a bacteria added to give it a tangy flavor. Add 1 tablespoon lemon juice to 1 cup milk, stir well, and allow it to stand for 5 minutes.

butternut squash   Both acorn squash and turban squash have a similar flavor as well as the blushing orange color of butternut and can be used interchangeably.

butterscotch   The difference between caramel and butterscotch is that butterscotch is made with light brown rather than granulated sugar. Substitute caramel sauce in direct proportion, or make your own sauce.

Yield: 1½ cups

1 cup firmly packed light brown sugar	2 tsp. cider vinegar
¼ cup light corn syrup	½ cup heavy cream
3 TB. water	1 tsp. pure vanilla extract
4 TB. unsalted butter, cut into small bits	

Combine brown sugar, corn syrup, and water in a small, heavy saucepan. Bring to a boil over medium heat, stirring occasionally, and boil without stirring until syrup reaches a golden brown. Remove the pan from the heat, and stir in butter and vinegar. Return the pan to the heat, and stir in cream and vanilla extract. Cook for 1 or 2 minutes or until thick and bubbly. Cool sauce to room temperature and then refrigerate sauce, tightly covered.

cabbage, green   Great both cooked and raw, cabbage is always in season. You'll find two types of green cabbage, the common cabbage and savoy cabbage that has wrinkled leaves, and both can be used interchangeably. Other alternatives are Brussels sprouts and Napa cabbage, which has a much milder flavor.

cabbage, red   The only vegetable that replicates the blushing red color of red cabbage is beets, so if the color is important that's the answer. If color isn't a factor, sub any of the green cabbages.

Cabernet Franc (*cah-ber-net frahc*)   *See* wine, red.

Cabernet Sauvignon (*cah-ber-net saw-ven-yohn*)   *See* wine, red.

cactus leaf   *See* nopale.

cactus pear   *See* prickly pear.

Caerphilly cheese   *See* cheese.

Cajun seasoning   Sometimes also called Creole seasoning, this seasoning is a preblended mix of spices. There's no one formula, and most contain both onion powder and garlic powder. I omit those ingredients and instead use fresh garlic and onion.

   ¹/₂ cup Cajun seasoning = 3 TB. kosher salt + 2 TB. paprika + 1 TB. cayenne + 1 TB. freshly ground black pepper + 1 TB. dried oregano + 1 TB. dried thyme

cake flour   *See* flour.

calamari (*cal-a-MAHR-ee*)   *See* squid.

California Jack   *See* cheese.

California red *See* chilies, fresh.

Calvados (*kal-vah-doze*) *See* brandy.

Campari (*kam-PAH-ri*) *See* wine, apéritif.

Canadian bacon *See* bacon, Canadian.

Canadian whisky *See* spirits.

cane syrup This viscous and very sweet syrup is made from ground sugar cane. Light corn syrup can be used instead.

cannellini bean (*can-el-LEAN-ee*) *See* beans, dried.

canola oil *See* fats and oils.

cantaloupe *See* melon.

capellini (*kah-peh-LEE-knee*) *See* pasta, dried.

capers Capers, pickled berries from a Mediterranean shrub, have a salty and piquant flavor. Chopped brine-cured green olives deliver the same flavor.

capon *See* chicken.

carambola (*car-em-BOW-la*) *See* star fruit.

caramel sauce Caramel is simply sugar and water cooked to a high temperature. Once that's done, just add some butter and cream, and you've got caramel sauce.

Yield: 1½ cups

1½ cups granulated sugar
½ cup water
3 TB. unsalted butter

1 cup heavy cream
1 tsp. pure vanilla extract

Combine sugar and water in a saucepan, and bring to a boil over medium-high heat. Swirl the pan by the handle but do not stir. Allow syrup to cook until it reaches a walnut brown color, swirling the pot by the handle frequently. Remove the pan from the heat, and stir in butter and cream with a long-handled spoon; the mixture will bubble

continues

continued

> furiously at first. Return the pan to low heat and stir until lumps have
> melted and sauce is smooth. Stir in vanilla extract, and transfer
> to a jar. Serve hot, at room temperature, or cold; sauce can be
> refrigerated for up to 1 week.

caraway seed   These tiny elliptical seeds give rye bread its characteristic
flavor. Peppery dill seed or licorice-tasting fennel seed are similar in flavor.
Or you can use Kümmel, a caraway-flavored liqueur and subtract the
Kümmel from the appropriate amount of liquid specified in the recipe.

cardamom seed   While these pods are used primarily in both Indian
and Scandinavian cooking, their flavor is like a cross between ginger
and cinnamon. Substitute those two spices in equal proportion for
cardamom.

cardoon   A vegetable popular with Mediterranean cuisines, cardoons
look like a bunch of wide celery. A combination of celery and artichoke
hearts replicates the flavor.

carnaroli rice (*can-ah-ROLL-ey*)   *See* rice.

carob   This powder made from the pulp of a tropical tree is sweet and
tastes somewhat like chocolate, so try ground bittersweet chocolate in its
place.

carp   This mild-tasting fish found in rivers, streams, and lakes looks
like a giant goldfish. Pike or whitefish are the best choices if it's not
available; both have the same delicate flavor and texture.

carrot   Carrots are a sweet root vegetable that play a supporting role
in most of the world's cuisines. If color isn't important, parsnips have a
similar flavor; if you're after the bright orange hue, substitute puréed
butternut squash or pumpkin.

casaba   *See* melon.

cascabel (*KAS-cah-bell*)   *See* chilies, dried.

cashew nut   The slightly sweet, buttery flavor of cashew nuts is similar
to macadamia or Brazil nuts.

cassava (*kuh-SAH-vah*)   *See* yucca.

castor (or **caster**) **sugar**   *See* sugar.

catfish   The sweet flavor of catfish has led to its increased popularity, and tilapia or sole are the best substitutions.

cauliflower   As a member of the cabbage family, its closest flavor cousin is broccoli. For a lighter shade and similar flavor, blanch green cabbage and treat it like cauliflower.

cavatappi (*kah-vah-TAH-pee*)   *See* pasta, dried.

caviar   When people think of caviar, what comes to mind are the prized salted sturgeon roe; depending on the species, they're labeled beluga, ossetra, or sevruga. All are now banned from importation because the prized fish from the Caspian Sea are endangered species. You can find roe from other fish; American sturgeon caviar is a good alternative. American red salmon caviar is frequently used as a garnish for foods, as is golden caviar extracted from native whitefish. In Japanese cooking, both capelin roe and flying fish roe (also called *tobiko*) are frequently used as garnish for sushi. Lobster coral is an alternative to these bright red forms of caviar.

cayenne (*KAY-yehn*)   Cayenne is the ground powder made from blending a number of hot chilies. Increase the amount of black or white pepper used by 25 percent, or add hot red pepper sauce along with black or white pepper.

celeriac   This knobby brown vegetable, also called celery root, is crunchy when raw and silky when cooked. It can range in size from an orange to a small head of cabbage. Use celery for salads, and cook parsnips or rutabagas for a purée, adding 1 teaspoon celery seed per pound of other vegetable.

celery   For a crunchy accent in salads, use fresh fennel stalks, although they'll add a slight licorice flavor. If the celery is to be braised, use Belgian endive.

celery root   *See* celeriac.

celery seed   Tiny and dark brown, celery seeds deliver a far more powerful flavor than fresh celery. For 1 teaspoon celery seed, substitute ¼ cup chopped celery leaves or 1 teaspoon dill seed.

cellophane noodles   Pale in tone and translucent, these threadlike noodles are made from the starch of mung beans. While there's no other mung bean product, very thin rice noodles or angel hair pasta, both of which need cooking, are good choices.

cèpe   *See* mushroom, wild.

Chablis (*sha-blee*)   *See* wine, white.

challah (*HAL-lah*)   What distinguishes this Jewish ceremonial bread usually baked as a braided oval is the high number of eggs it contains. French brioche is the best substitute, although it contains a significant amount of butter, too.

chalupas (*cha-LOO-pahs*)   These Mexican breads are made with cornmeal, so corn tortillas, although thinner, are the best alternative; and they're easier to find, too.

Chambord (*cham-boord*)   *See* liqueur.

champagne   *See* wine, sparkling.

chanterelles (*chan-ter-elles*)   *See* mushroom, wild.

chardonnay (*char-doon-ay*)   *See* wine, white.

Châteauneuf-du-Pape (*shah-tow-nhuef due pahp*)   *See* wine, red.

chayote (*chi-YOT-tea*)   Chayote, also called mirliton, is a pear-shaped fruit with a light green skin. Cooked, its bland flavor is similar to both zucchini and crookneck squash, so they're your best alternatives.

cheddar cheese   *See* cheese.

cheese   Thousands of cheeses are produced around the world; that's why you find hundreds of references in this book leading you to this single entry. Cheeses fall into families, and it's possible to substitute one for another easily using the following tables.

The critical factors in determining the distinctive character of each cheese are the kind of milk used (cow, sheep, goat) and its fat content, the coagulation methods, cutting, cooking, forming of the curd, the type of culture, salting, and the ripening method. Cheeses are divided by their texture and, in some cases, flavor.

blue-veined cheese White- to creamy-colored cheeses with blue-veined interiors have a tangy, piquant flavor. The cheeses get the blue veins via skewers that have been inoculated with a starter bacteria and are then run through the cheese. Blue-veined cheeses are often served crumbled in salads or complementing fruits—pears, in particular. Their texture varies from creamy to crumbly, and those of a lesser quality may be overly salty.

Blue-Veined Cheeses at a Glance

Cheese	Origin	Milk	Flavor
Bleu de Bresse	France	cow/goat	piquant and peppery
Danish Blue	Denmark	cow	piquant and tangy
Gorgonzola	Italy	cow/goat	piquant and peppery
Maytag Blue	USA	cow	piquant and tangy
Roquefort	France	sheep	sharp and spicy
Stilton	England	cow	piquant and spicy

hard cheese Maturity is critical for the flavor of hard cheese. The more expensive cheeses tend to have been stored longer, creating a better-quality cheese. Almost like wine, hard cheeses are "aged" in cellars for years.

Hard Cheeses at a Glance

Cheese	Origin	Milk	Flavor
Cheddar	USA	cow	mild to sharp
Cheshire	England	cow	mild to tangy
Colby	USA	cow	mild to mellow
Emmenthaler	Switzerland	cow	mild, sweet, nutty
Gloucester	England	cow	slightly sharp
Gruyére	Switzerland	cow	mild and sweet

continues

Hard Cheeses at a Glance   (continued)

Cheese	Origin	Milk	Flavor
Jarlsberg	Switzerland	cow	mild and sweet
Kassseri	Greece	sheep	sharp and piquant
Leister	England	cow	mild to sharp
Parmesan	Italy	cow	sharp and piquant
Provolone	Italy	cow	bland acid flavor
Romano	Italy	cow/goat	sharp and piquant
Sap Sago	Switzerland	cow	sharp and pungent
Swiss	USA	cow	sweet and nutty
Tillamook	USA	cow	mild to mellow

semi-soft cheese   Firmer than soft cheeses, semi-soft cheeses do not require a sharp knife for cutting. Semi-softs come in a great variety of shapes, sizes, and flavors.

Semi-Soft Cheeses at a Glance

Cheese	Origin	Milk	Flavor
American	USA	cow	mild
Asadero	Mexico	cow	mild
Asiago	Italy	cow	piquant, sharp
Bel Paese	Italy	cow	mild to robust
Edam	Holland	cow	mild
Feta	Greece	sheep	salty, sharp
Fontina	Italy	cow	mild and nutty
Gouda	Holland	cow	mild, like Edam
Havarti	Denmark	cow	mild, frequently flavored

Cheese	Origin	Milk	Flavor
Jack (also called California Jack and Monterey Jack)	USA	cow	mild to mellow
Manchego	Spain	sheep	mild to mellow
Mozzarella (also called buffalo mozzarella if made with buffalo milk)	Italy	cow	mild and delicate
Muenster	Germany	cow	mild to mellow
Port-Salut	France	cow	mild to robust
Raclette	Switzerland	cow	full and fruity
Taleggio	Italy	cow	mild to mellow

soft cheese   Soft cheeses melt very easily and evenly when heated. They are perfect as a layer or topping in a baked dish.

Soft Cheeses at a Glance

Cheese	Origin	Milk	Flavor
Boursault	France	cow	mild to strong
Boursin	France	cow	mild (sometimes with herbs)
Brie	France	cow	mild to pungent
Brillat-Savarin	France	cow	mild, slightly sweet
Bûcheron	France	goat	mild to mellow
Camembert	France	cow	mild to pungent
Crottin	France	goat	sharp

continues

Soft Cheeses at a Glance   (continued)

Cheese	Origin	Milk	Flavor
Explorateur	France	cow	very creamy, mild
Limburger	Belgium	cow	strong, aromatic
Montrachet	France	goat	mild
Saint Andre	France	cow	mild to tangy
Vacherin	Switzerland	cow	mild to pungent

Chenin Blanc (*che-nohn blahn*)   *See* wine, white.

cherimoya (*cherry-MOY-ya*)   The creamy texture of this tropical fruit with patterned skin is like that of a banana, but the flavor also has some nuances of pineapple and papaya. Use a combination of the three fruits, puréed together.

cherry, dried   Dried cranberries have a similar flavor as well as color.

cherry, fresh   Sweet cherries are a summer treat, and their flavor is really like no other fruit. If you want a red color, dice up fresh plums.

Cherry Heering   *See* liqueur.

Cherry Marnier   *See* liqueur.

cherrystone clam   *See* clam.

chervil   This lacy-leafed member of the parsley clan has a slight anise flavor, but not as strong as that of tarragon. Use one part tarragon and three parts parsley to replicate chervil.

chestnut   With a mild and nutty flavor, it's hard to substitute for chestnuts, and luckily, they now come vacuum-packed and canned, so there's no need to wait for their fall season. Macadamia nuts or Brazil nuts have a similar flavor although not the same starchy texture.

Chianti (*kee-AHN-tee*)   *See* wine, red.

chick pea (or **garbanzo bean**)   *See* beans, dried.

chicken   The advances in poultry processing in tandem with our desire to reduce the saturated fat in our diets has led us to become a chicken-eating country. When you're picking chicken, look for packages that do not have an accumulation of liquid in the bottom. That can be a sign that the chicken has been frozen and thawed. Most chickens we see at the market are termed *fryers*, although they can be cooked by any cooking method. Fryers are also cut up by part. The following table serves as a guide to chicken and its feathered cousins.

Chicken at a Glance

Bird	Description	Weight
Broiler	Very tender	1½ to 2 lb.
Capon	Castrated rooster, very tender, best roasted	5 to 8 lb.
Fryer	Very tender	2½ to 4 lb.
Poussin	Very tender	¾ to 1 lb.
Roaster	Best roasted, breast can be done as slices	4 to 8 lb.
Rock Cornish hen	Very tender	1 to 2 lb.
Stewing hen (also called stewing fowl)	Tough, needs braising	4 to 6 lb.

Another quandary when cooking chicken is when you change from a boneless cut to one with bones, or vice versa. The following table helps you determine how much you'll need.

Per Person Chicken Amounts

Cut	With Bone	Without Bone
Broiler	½ per person	n/a
Capon	⅙ to ⅛	n/a
Cornish hen	1 per person if small ½ if large	n/a
Fryer	¼ per person	n/a

continues

Per Person Chicken Amounts (continued)

Cut	With Bone	Without Bone
Fryer breast	½ whole breast	6 to 8 oz.
Fryer leg	2 per person	n/a
Fryer thigh	2 per person	6 to 8 oz.
Poussin	1 per person	n/a
Roaster	⅙ to ⅛	n/a
Stewing hen	¼ to ⅙	n/a

You can substitute any fryer piece for any other. If a recipe calls for chicken breasts and you're using dark meat, add 5 to 7 minutes to the cooking time; in reverse, subtract 5 minutes.

Turkey cutlets can be substituted for boneless, skinless chicken breasts in any recipe, and the finished dish will probably have a richer flavor. Veal scallops can also be substituted for pounded chicken breasts; they will be as delicate, and the meal will be more elegant. Sauté them just for 2 or 3 minutes on a side.

Halved Rock Cornish hens can be used in recipes in place of fryer pieces; because the hen is smaller, the cooking time will be the same, even though the individual piece will be larger.

Toque Tips

Always store chicken on the bottom shelf of the refrigerator. Should any juices escape from the package, they won't drip down onto and contaminate other foods.

chicory   *See* lettuce.

chili oil   Originally used in Asian cooking, many Latin American recipes also now specify this oil infused with hot chili peppers that turn it a bright orange. Add cayenne or hot red pepper sauce to taste instead. Or combine 1 cup vegetable oil with ¼ cup crushed red pepper flakes in a saucepan. Heat over medium heat for 10 minutes, remove the pan from the heat, and allow the mixture to steep for at least 1 day before using. Strain out and discard the solids, and store the oil in the refrigerator.

chili powder This backbone of Southwestern cooking is one of our oldest herb and spice blends.

½ cup chili powder = 2 TB. ground red chili + 2 TB. paprika + 1 TB. ground coriander + 1 TB. garlic powder + 1 TB. onion powder + 2 tsp. ground cumin + 2 tsp. cayenne + 2 tsp. dried oregano

chili sauce This chunky condiment is a blending of tomatoes, sweet chilies, onions, green peppers, vinegar, sugar, and spices. Although the texture will be smooth, ketchup is the best replacement.

chilies, dried As is true with sun-dried tomatoes, the flavor of a dried chili pepper is more concentrated than when it's fresh. And as a general rule, the smaller the pepper, the hotter the pepper. Here are some of the main species of chilies you'll find dried:

ancho Dried poblano chilies, anchos come from California (where they're sometimes incorrectly called pasilla chilies) and Mexico and range from dark red to almost black. They're about 4½ inches long and 3 inches wide, are moderately hot, with a smoky undertaste. They're wrinkled but should still be pliable. Pasilla chilies, although difficult to find, may be substituted.

cascabel Meaning jingle or sleigh bells, cascabels are roughly shaped 1½-inch brownish-brick red spheres and have seeds rattling inside. They are moderately hot and only available dried.

chipotle These are jalapeño chilies that have been dried, smoked, and often pickled. Chipotles are usually a dark shade of brown and have a very hot smoky taste. They are frequently packed in a spicy sauce and sold canned as chipotles in adobo sauce.

mulato This chili is the same shape as the ancho, but it's darker and sweeter in flavor, more earthy than hot. Ancho is the best substitution.

pasilla Named for *pasa*, which means "raisin" in Spanish, this chili is also called chilaca when fresh, brown, and ripe, and negro when dried and black. Pasillas are mild to hot in temperature, are used in molé, and may be substituted with ancho or mulatto chilies.

pequín   These small dried red chilies are shaped like an elongated sphere and are extremely hot. Also called chilepequeno, bird pepper, petrine, and chiltecpin, pequins grow wild in Mexico, the Caribbean, and along the U.S. border, but few are harvested and they are quite expensive. Cayenne may be substituted.

tepín   These are a small round version of the pequin, and they look like a large red peppercorn. Pequins or cascabels may be substituted.

chilies, fresh   With the popularity of Asian and Hispanic cuisines, as well as the use of chilies in many regions of American cooking, chilies are frequently called for in recipes, both in their fresh and dried forms. There are hundreds of varieties of chilies in the world, all native to the Americas.

Chilies vary greatly in their hotness from pepper to pepper. It's best to start by adding only a portion of the chilies specified in a recipe and then continue adding until you reach the level of heat you like.

Some Asian recipes call for only the stem to be discarded and the entire pepper including ribs and seeds to be used, but most American and Hispanic recipes assume that the seeds and ribs have been discarded, unless otherwise specified.

These are the species most often specified in recipes:

Anaheim   Also called California, California greens, chilies verdes, or (when canned) mild green chilies, Anaheim chilies are dark green, about 7 inches long and 1½ inches wide, with a mild to moderate flavor. When the chilies ripen completely in the fall, they turn red, sweet, and mild. Anaheim's large size makes them ideal for stuffing. Poblanos may be substituted.

California red   Also called red chilies or Colorado chilies, these are ripened green Anaheim chilies that have turned red. Relatively smooth and shiny, California red chilies are often strung to make decorative ristras. Spiciness ranges from mild to hot.

Fresno   This bright red chili has a sweet component to balance the heat. They are approximately 2 inches long. Jalapeño can be substituted, but use less because a green jalapeño is generally hotter.

guero   Also called Hungarian yellow wax chili, this hot yellow or yellow-green chili is similar in shape to the jalapeño. It turns red when ripe.

habañero　These are at the top of the heat scale, but in a small quantity, they have an almost fruity flavor. Scotch bonnet is the best substitution, and if you're using either jalapeño or serrano, increase the amount by 50 percent.

hot cherry　Also called Hungarian cherry pepper, bird cherry, or Creole cherry pepper, hot cherry peppers are up to 2 inches wide. But watch out: this spherical chili can be very hot. It can be used when dark green, but it's best when it's completely ripe and red. Cayenne, sandia, or Mexican improved chilies may be substituted.

jalapeño　A fairly small, dark green hot chili approximately 2 inches long and 1 inch wide, jalapeños are one of the most widely available fresh chilies. Serranos are a common substitution, although the heat from jalapeños is immediate while the serrano provides more of an afterburn. Jalapeños can vary in the level of hotness, and those with striations on the skin are older and usually hotter.

New Mexico green　New Mexico green chilies are similar to the Anaheim chili, but shorter and more potent. Either Anaheims or poblanos can be substituted with great success.

New Mexico red　Also called chilies de ristra, New Mexico red chilies are long and shiny peppers and used to make decorative wreaths. New Mexico chili powder is made from ground, dried New Mexico red chilies. While no other red chilies have the same mild flavor, you can substitute a New Mexico green, Anaheim, or poblano.

pepperoncini　These are sometimes sold as Tuscan peppers and are frequently either roasted or pickled and served as part of an antipasto. They're bright red, thin, and 2 to 3 inches long. Although larger, New Mexico reds are the best alternative for red pepper with the same slightly sweet and fairly mild flavor.

poblano　Large, tapered, shiny dark green chilies about 4 inches long and 2½ inches wide, poblanos are mild to hot. When used in sauces, they may be interchanged with Anaheim green chilies, although the flavor will be different. If you're desperate, green bell peppers can be substituted for stuffed poblanos, but increase the spice level of the filling.

Scotch bonnet   These peppers native to Jamaica give jerk its jolt. It looks like, and tastes like, a habañero but it's a bit smaller. You can also substitute a jalapeño or serrano.

serrano   Serranos are tapered, thin, bright-green chilies similar to but smaller than jalapeños and often pickled or canned in oil. Good for cooking or as a garnish, serranos vary in hotness as much as a jalapeño. Jalapeño chilies may be substituted.

Thai   These very powerful chilies are about 1 inch long, slender, and dark green or deep red. Cayennes or serranos may be substituted.

Jalapeño and serrano chilies are almost universally available in supermarkets, and they can be used in place of any hot chili in a recipe to create heat. Bell peppers can be used for stuffing, if Anaheim or poblano are not available.

In a pinch, dried chili flakes, ground cayenne, or red pepper sauce can be used for the desired effect. Use sweet red or green bell pepper in the recipe and then add one of these substitutions to the level you wish. However, do not use commercial chili powder, because it contains many other spices and flavors.

Chinese cabbage   *See* bok choy.

Chinese chili paste with garlic   Available in the Asian section of most groceries, this thick paste is made with fermented fava beans, chilies, and garlic. A mixture of hot red pepper sauce and fresh garlic simulates the taste.

Chinese five-spice powder   It's actually easier to find this mix than it is to find some of its component ingredients in supermarkets, but if you need to make it yourself, it's equal parts ground cinnamon, ground cloves, ground fennel seed, ground star anise, and ground Szechwan peppercorns.

Chinese parsley   *See* cilantro.

chipotle chili (*chi-POHT-lay*)   *See* chilies, dried.

chives   The green tops from scallions, finely chopped, give you the same onion flavor and green color.

chocolate   The key to all chocolate desserts is to use a high-quality product, and with the following exceptions, to use the type of chocolate specified in a recipe. The amount of additional sugar and other ingredients are calculated according to the sweetness level of the chocolate. Here is a guide to chocolate:

bittersweet   This chocolate is slightly sweetened with sugar, and the amount varies depending on the manufacturer. This chocolate must contain 35 percent chocolate liquor, and it should be used when intense chocolate taste is desired. It can also be used interchangeably with semisweet chocolate in cooking and baking.

Dutch process cocoa powder   This is a type of cocoa powder formulated with reduced acidity, and it gives foods a mellower flavor. However, it also burns at a lower temperature than more common cocoa.

milk   This is a mild-flavored chocolate used primarily for candy bars but rarely (except for milk chocolate chips) in cooking. It can have as little as 10 percent chocolate liquor, but must contain 12 percent milk solids.

semisweet   This chocolate is sweetened with sugar, but unlike bittersweet, it also can have additional flavorings such as vanilla. It is available in bar form as well as chips and pieces.

1 oz. semisweet chocolate = 1 oz. unsweetened chocolate + 4 tsp. granulated sugar

unsweetened   Also referred to as baking or bitter chocolate, this is the purest of all cooking chocolate. It is hardened chocolate liquor (the essence of the cocoa bean, not an alcohol) that contains no sugar. It's usually packaged in a bar of eight 1-ounce blocks.

1 oz. unsweetened chocolate = 3 TB. cocoa powder + 1 TB. vegetable shortening

unsweetened cocoa powder   This is powdered chocolate that has had a portion of the cocoa butter removed. Cocoa keeps indefinitely in a cool place.

white chocolate   Actually ivory in color, white chocolate is technically not chocolate at all; it's made from cocoa butter, sugar, and flavoring. It's difficult to work with and should be used in recipes that are specifically designed for it. Do not substitute it for other types of chocolate in a recipe.

Bittersweet, semisweet, and sweet chocolate can be used interchangeably in recipes, depending on personal taste. Because most chocolate desserts tend to be sweet, it's better to go from a semisweet to a bittersweet than the other direction. Chocolate chips and bits of broken chocolate should not be substituted for one another. Chocolate chips are formulated to retain their shape at high heat. They react differently than chopped chocolate when baked and can form gritty granules in a cooled dessert.

chorizo (*chore-EAT-zoh*)   This highly spiced pork sausage is often used in Mexican and Spanish cuisines. Portuguese linguiça or Cajun andouille have similar flavors.

chubs   *See* whitefish.

chuck   *See* beef.

chutney   Used as a condiment with Indian curries, chutney can contain a number of fruits and/or vegetables, and it has a sweet-sour-hot profile. To substitute, combine 1 cup orange marmalade or apricot jam with ¼ cup cider vinegar, and season with hot red pepper sauce. Or purée 1 cup mango salsa and add cider vinegar and hot red pepper sauce to taste.

ciabatta (*chi-BAT-tah*)   This light-textured Italian bread has a crispy crust. Any unflavored French or Italian bread can be used in its place.

cider vinegar   *See* vinegar.

cilantro   The world is divided into people who like or loathe cilantro. This first cousin to parsley has a very complex and distinct flavor. Flat-leaf parsley is the best substitute; add ½ teaspoon ground cumin per 2 tablespoons chopped fresh parsley to add more flavor.

cinnamon   This most common of the baking spices is also used in savory cooking in Greece and a few other cuisines. For each 1 teaspoon cinnamon, substitute ½ teaspoon allspice and a pinch of ground nutmeg.

cipollini (*chi-poh-LEEN-ni*)   These mildly flavored onions are squat in appearance and about 2 inches in diameter. White boiling onions can be cooked the same way.

clam   These muscular mollusks range from quarter size in the North Atlantic to 2 pounds in the Pacific. They are categorized by whether they are hard shells that are firmly closed or soft shells that have a tail extending outward; their shells are not actually soft, but brittle. What to substitute depends on how the clams are to be eaten:

for chowders   Chowders are traditionally made from large, hard-shelled clams called quahogs that are more than 4 inches in diameter and far too tough to eat on the half shell. Most seafood departments now carry fresh minced clams for this purpose, or you can use canned clams.

on the half shell   Only hard-shelled clams are eaten raw. Littlenecks are 2 inches or less in diameter, Topnecks are 2 to 3 inches, and cherrystones are larger than 3 inches. Any of these can be substituted for each other, although the littlenecks are the most prized. Oysters can also be eaten this way.

steamed   Steamers are small, soft-shelled clams, but either littlenecks or cherrystones can be steamed. Mussels steam well, too.

Toque Tips

There's a ritual to eating genuine steamer clams because they're usually gritty—and they're definitely finger food. Pour some of the cooking broth into a cup, and with your fingers, pull off the covering on the clam's "tail." Then dip the clam into the broth to remove residual sand and then into melted butter.

clarified butter   *See* butter, clarified.

clementine   A member of the mandarin orange family with a loose skin and sweet flavor, any mandarin or common navel oranges can be substituted for the delicate clementine.

clotted cream   An English specialty served at tea time, clotted cream is made by removing the thick cream layer from unpasteurized milk. To substitute the same texture, whip heavy cream until soft, but not stiff, peaks form.

clove   With their spicy and pungent flavor and aroma, cloves are used in both sweet and savory dishes. Use a pinch each of allspice, nutmeg, and black pepper for each ¼ teaspoon ground cloves.

cocktail sauce   This dipping sauce for cold crustaceans is found in every market; its main ingredient is chili sauce.

Yield: 1 cup

¾ cup chili sauce (or ketchup)
3 TB. prepared horseradish or
  to taste

2 TB. freshly squeezed lemon
  juice
Hot red pepper sauce

Stir together chili sauce, horseradish, and lemon juice, and season with hot red pepper sauce. Sauce can be refrigerated for up to 1 week.

---

cocoa powder   *See* chocolate.

coconut   Many whole foods markets now sell unsweetened shredded coconut, which can be substituted for fresh grated in direct proportion. If all you can find is sweetened coconut, soak it in boiling water for 10 minutes to remove at least some of the sugar and then delete the sugar in a recipe calling for unsweetened.

coconut milk   The liquid inside a fresh coconut is not coconut milk. To make coconut milk, combine equal parts grated, unsweetened coconut and boiling water in a blender on high speed. Strain off the coconut milk and discard the solids.

cod   Cod actually refers to a family of several related species, all which have lean, flaky flesh that's white when cooked and mild in flavor. Here are the main varieties:

Atlantic cod   The most common cod, it can run from less than 10 pounds to more than 25 pounds, and has firm, sweet, white flesh that flakes when cooked.

cusk   Relatively unknown outside of New England, cusk has firm, white flesh, similar to Atlantic cod, with a strip of bones that must be removed. Usually sold as fillet, cusk can be prepared using the same methods as for Atlantic cod.

haddock   A somewhat smaller fish than the Atlantic cod, haddock usually weigh 2 to 5 pounds. The flesh is slightly softer and finer and has a more delicate flavor. Because haddock does not take salt as well as other cod, haddock is cured by drying and smoking. Finnan haddie is split smoked haddock. ("Haddie" is a nickname for haddock.)

hake　There are numerous species of hake, and most are smaller and more slender than the other cods. Most hake weigh less than 3 pounds, although the white hake can be as much as 50 pounds. Hake has off-white flesh, which has a slightly stronger flavor and fewer bones than other cods. Hake is sold fresh, whole, or in fillets. In the United States, silver, white, and squirrel hake are among the popular varieties.

pollock　Pollock is abundant throughout the Atlantic and generally runs 4 to 8 pounds, although it can weigh as much as 35 pounds. This fish suffers in popularity because the flesh is gray when raw but turns white as it cooks. Pollock has soft flesh and a bit more flavor than Atlantic cod and is usually much less expensive than other cods.

scrod　Scrod is not a species of fish, but has come to mean small Atlantic cod, haddock, or pollack. Usually less than 3 pounds, scrod has soft, delicate flesh that's sweeter than other cods. It's sold as fillets.

whiting　This fish is actually the silver hake or the New England hake and is delicious whole or as fillets. The flesh is off-white when raw but turns snowy white when cooked, and is softer and flakier than Atlantic cod. Whiting are smaller than other cods, usually about 12 or 13 inches, and a mere 1 pound in weight.

In addition to substituting any of these species for each other, halibut and whitefish are good alternatives.

cognac (*kon-yak*)　*See* brandy.

Cointreau (*kwan-trow*)　*See* liqueur.

collards　*See* greens.

Comice pear (*ko-mees*)　*See* pear.

conch (*konk*)　The tough flesh of this beautiful mollusk is hard to find out of the tropics and must always be tenderized. Minced clams are the best substitute and have a similarly delicate flavor.

conchiglie (*kohn-CHEE-l'yeh*)　*See* pasta, dried.

confectioners' sugar　*See* sugar.

consommé   *See* stock.

converted rice   *See* rice.

coriander, fresh   *See* cilantro.

coriander seed   Both fresh cilantro leaves and these tiny seeds, most often used ground in both Scandinavian and Middle Eastern food, come from the same plant in the parsley family. A combination of crushed caraway seeds and ground cumin is the best you can do to replicate the aromatic and somewhat strong flavor.

corn   Corn is actually a relative of the sweet pea, which is why eating it fresh before the sugar is converted to starch is so important. Any species of fresh corn tastes similar, and frozen corn can be substituted. For a purée, try sweet peas for a subtle and sweet flavor or yellow squash for a food with the same color.

1 (10-oz.) pkg. frozen corn = 2 cups corn kernels (4 ears)

corn oil   *See* fats and oils.

corn syrup, dark   Corn syrup, extremely sweet, is made by processing cornstarch with various other ingredients; the dark variety has a caramel flavor. To substitute, mix ¾ cup light corn syrup with ¼ cup molasses for 1 cup. Or combine 1½ cups firmly packed dark brown sugar with ⅓ cup water in a small saucepan. Bring to a boil and cook until sugar is dissolved and mixture thickens.

corn syrup, light   To replicate 1 cup of this viscous clear liquid, boil 1¼ cups granulated sugar with ½ cup water until it's thick.

corned beef   This brisket of beef has been cured in a salty solution for more than a week with herbs and spices before it's cooked. For a sandwich, pastrami or ham has a similar salty flavor.

cornichon (*kor-knee-shown*)   Any sweet gherkin pickle has the same flavor as these tiny French pickles traditionally served with pâté and cold meats.

Cornish hen   *See* chicken.

cornmeal   The corn we eat off the cob is a different variety from the one that's dried and ground into cornmeal, and the different dried corn products depend on what other ingredients are added during the processing.

Dried Corn at a Glance

Corn	Texture	Uses
Cornmeal	medium to fine ground hulled kernels	baked goods, batters, coatings for fried foods
Grits	cracked hominy	hot cereal, side dishes
Hominy	whole, hulled kernels soaked in lye	stews, side dishes
Masa Harina	corn processed with lime to remove the hulls and then ground fine	tortillas and other Mexican dishes
Polenta	a coarse cornmeal	porridge, baked goods

cornstarch (or **cornflour**)   Made from the endosperm portion of the corn kernel, cornstarch is a great thickening agent, and should always be mixed with cold water to prevent lumping.

1 TB. cornstarch = 1 TB. arrowroot, 2 TB. instant tapioca (for fruit pies), or 2 TB. instant mashed potato flakes (for soups)

cottage cheese   Cottage cheese comes in small-, medium-, and large-curd versions and also with a different percentage of butterfat, depending on the milk it's made from. Ricotta cheese is almost identical in appearance and very similar in flavor.

cottonseed oil   *See* fats and oils.

coulis (*koo-lee*)   This is the French term for any thick fruit or vegetable purée. Strained baby food is already the proper consistency, or you can purée frozen dry-pack fruits or vegetables.

country ham   *See* ham.

court-bouillon (*core boo-yawn*)   This is the herbed vegetable stock used for poaching fish, and any vegetable stock can be substituted.

couscous   Not a grain, although often mistaken for one, couscous is a granular pasta made from semolina. No other pasta cooks as quickly or has the same texture, so use a grain such as buckwheat or finely ground bulgur. The cooking times will be longer.

crab Containers of crabmeat, already picked from the shells, are one of the greatest convenience foods of all time, and any of the other crustaceans such as shrimp or lobster can be substituted as can imitation crab (surimi). If you want to cook a soft-shelled crab, there's no exact substitute, but thin, mild fish fillets like tilapia cook in the same amount of time.

crab boil This blend of herbs and spices is used to flavor crabs and other shellfish while they cook. Pickling spices have almost the same ingredients. Create your own mixture and tie it in cheesecloth before adding it to the pot.

> *$^1\!/_2$ cup crab boil = 6 small whole red chilies + 2 crushed bay leaves + 1 TB. black peppercorns + 1 TB. coriander seeds + 1 TB. whole cloves + 1 TB. mustard seeds + 1 TB. dill seeds + 1 whole allspice*

cranberry, dried Dried cranberries are always sold sweetened. Dried cherries have almost the same flavor, but they're not quite as tart.

cranberry, fresh Lip-puckering tart, fresh cranberries really have no substitute, so I suggest buying extra bags when they're in season in the fall and freezing them. Tart red currants are even harder to find, but sour cherries can be used in baking in the same way.

cranberry bean *See* beans, dried.

crawfish (or **crayfish**) These crustaceans are only about 2 inches long, and they resemble tiny lobsters. Only the tail meat is eaten, so small shrimp give you the same shape or chopped lobster meat provides a flavor that's closer.

cream What determines the name of cream is its butterfat content. Half-and-half is between 10.5 and 18 percent butterfat, light cream is between 18 and 30 percent, while whipping cream is between 30 and 36 percent, and heavy cream is 36 percent or higher. For cooking, it's easy to create the level of butterfat specified.

> *1 cup half-and-half = $^1\!/_2$ cup light cream + $^1\!/_2$ cup whole milk*
> *1 cup light cream = $^7\!/_8$ cup whole milk + 2 TB. melted butter*
> *1 cup heavy cream = $^3\!/_4$ cup whole milk + $^1\!/_3$ cup melted butter*

cream cheese   This all-American fresh cheese is used both as a spread—what would a bagel be without it?—and as an ingredient. French Neufchâtel is a good substitute, or you can make your own by combining equal parts ricotta and plain yogurt.

cream of tartar   Ground to a fine powder from the acid deposits left on the inside of wine barrels, cream of tartar is used to add volume to beaten egg whites and as a leavening agent in conjunction with baking soda. Salt performs the same function for egg whites, and you can use baking powder instead of the combination of baking soda and cream of tartar.

cream sauce   *See* white sauce.

crème fraîche (*krem fresh*)   This thickened cream has a tangy flavor similar to that of sour cream, but it can be boiled without curdling. If the dish is cold or only heated to a warm temperature, substitute sour cream in equal amounts. If the dish has to boil, make your own crème fraîche.

Yield: 1¼ cups

1 cup heavy cream   3 TB. plain yogurt

Warm cream and yogurt in a small saucepan over low heat until tepid; do not heat until hot. Remove the pan from heat and allow to sit at room temperature, loosely covered with plastic wrap, for 18 to 24 hours or until lightly thickened. The crème fraîche can be refrigerated for up to 1 week.

Variation: You can use a few tablespoons of a previous batch of crème fraîche as a starter for the next batch, or you can use sour cream or buttermilk as the starter.

---

crenshaw   *See* melon.

crimini   *See* mushroom, wild.

croaker   *See* drum.

crookneck squash   *See* yellow squash.

crostini (*crus-TEE-knee*)   These are thin slices of toast served with a variety of toppings, so any cracker or Melba toast can be used.

crottin (*crow-tan*)   *See* cheese.

crouton   These bits of crispy toast are a great way to top salads or soups. Break up tortilla chips, bagel chips, or crackers. Or cut bread into ¼- to ½-inch cubes, depending on how large you like them. Toss the cubes with olive oil or melted butter and the seasonings of your choice. It can be as simple as salt and freshly ground black pepper, or include minced garlic or dried herbs. Bake the cubes in a single layer on a cookie sheet in a 375°F oven for 6 to 10 minutes or until croutons are browned. When croutons are cool, store them in an airtight plastic bag for up to 1 week.

crumb crust   Graham crackers are traditionally used for the crusts for cheesecakes and key lime pies, but any chocolate or vanilla plain cookie works just as well: combine 2 cups crushed cookie crumbs with 6 tablespoons melted unsalted butter. You could also add 1 or 2 tablespoons granulated or dark brown sugar, ½ teaspoon ground cinnamon, or 1 teaspoon grated citrus zest. Pack the mixture into a 9-inch pie plate or into the bottom of a 10-inch springform pan.

cucumber   The mild flavor and crunchy texture of raw cucumber make celery or fennel the best substitute, although fennel has a slightly anise flavor. If the cucumber is to be cooked, use zucchini or chayote squash.

cumin seed   Cumin has a hot and somewhat bitter flavor, and the seeds should always be ground before use; that's why finding ground cumin is more common than its seeds. If you don't have cumin, grind ⅓ anise seed and ⅔ caraway seeds to a powder instead.

Curaçao (*cure-ah-SOW*)   *See* liqueur.

curly endive   *See* lettuce.

currant, dried   Made from zante grapes, dried currants are smaller and rounder than raisins. Raisins are the best choice.

curry powder Any particular curry powder, called garam masala in Indian groceries, is a blending of up to 20 spices. You can make it to suit your personal taste, too.

½ cup curry powder = 3 TB. ground coriander + 2 TB. crushed red pepper flakes + 2 TB. ground cumin + 2 TB. ground fenugreek seeds + 1 TB. ground ginger + 1 TB. turmeric + 1 TB. ground mustard seeds + 1 tsp. freshly ground black pepper + 1 tsp. ground cinnamon

cusk *See* cod.

daikon (*di-kon*) These huge Asian radishes, which can range in size from 6 to 12 inches long, have a slightly sweeter flavor than European red radishes, but those are the best substitute.

dal *See* lentils.

damson plum *See* plums.

dandelion greens *See* greens.

dashi (*dah-shee*) This popular fish-flavored Japanese stock is made with dried bonito tuna flakes. A combination of half vegetable stock and half seafood stock gives you about the same flavor.

dates You can only find fresh dates in the Middle East; good thing, because all our recipes call for dried ones. Chopped figs or raisins provide the same color and almost the same texture.

deer   *See* game meat.

Delmonico steak   *See* beef.

Dijon mustard (*dee-john*)   *See* mustard.

dill seed   Dill pickles wouldn't be dill pickles without dill seed, but a combination of crushed caraway seeds and celery seeds approximates the flavor.

dill weed   Dried dill weed is no substitute for the flavor and slightly citrus aroma of the fresh version. If using dill weed for garnish, fennel leaves look almost identical; in cooking, use a combination of fresh tarragon and parsley to add the appropriate flavor.

Toque Tips

The freshness of dill is an excellent balance to the saltiness of smoked fish and the oiliness of fish like salmon.

ditalini (*dee-tah-LEE-knee*)   *See* pasta, dried.

dogfish   *See* shark.

Dolcetto (*dole-CHE-toh*)   *See* wine, red.

dolphin   *See* mahi mahi.

Dover sole   Flounder and tilapia are the best substitutes for this delicately flavored flatfish native to the North Atlantic.

draft beer   *See* beer.

Drambuie   *See* liqueur.

drum   This family of fish found in temperate waters has firm flesh and is low in fat. Small drums are sometimes called croakers, sea trout, or redfish; substitute grouper, snapper, kingfish, or white seabass.

dry mustard   *See* mustard.

Dubonnet (*doo-bone-ay*)   *See* wine, apéritif.

duck   The best substitute for duck is goose. Both have a slightly gamey flavor and only dark meat. Geese are generally larger, so cooking times will vary. To eliminate the gamey flavor, use turkey or chicken thighs, but don't substitute white meat poultry for this dark meat bird.

Toque Tips

If you want to get all the fat out from under the skin of a duck or goose, prick the skin horizontally with a metal skewer before you put it in the oven. The fat will melt and drain away from the skin and the meat won't dry out.

duck fat   In France, duck fat is used as a cooking medium because of the flavor it adds to foods and its high smoke point. Chicken fat or vegetable oil are the best substitutes.

durian   This fruit from Malaysia has a foul smell, but its creamy flesh has a rich texture and sweet flavor. Cherimoya or banana with some pineapple added approaches the flavor.

Edam (*E-dam*)   *See* cheese.

edamame (*en-dah-mah-me*)   There's no question that soybeans, or edamame as the Japanese call them, are a wonder food. Most whole food markets now carry fresh soybeans, and they're available frozen almost everywhere. Baby lima beans, green peas, and garbanzo beans are the best substitutes.

eel   Eels are firm and meaty, with a high fat content and rich flavor, and they are really unique among aquatic species. Bluefish and mackerel have a similar flavor.

egg   The size of eggs (jumbo, extra large, large, medium, and small) is determined by how much the eggs weigh per dozen. Most cookbooks specify large eggs, so if you're using small eggs, increase the number by 1 for every 4 large eggs specified in a recipe. If you're using medium eggs, increase the number by 1 for every 6 large eggs. On the other side, decrease the number of eggs called for by 1 for every 4 jumbo eggs used and by 1 for every 8 extra large eggs used.

½ egg = 1½ TB. whole egg, lightly beaten, or 2 quail eggs

1 whole egg = 3 TB. mayonnaise for baking, 2½ TB. powdered egg + 2 TB. water, 2 egg yolks + 1 TB. water (for richer baked goods), or ¼ cup egg substitute

2 whole eggs = 1 whole egg + 2 egg whites to cut cholesterol

Toque Tips

If you want to see how fresh your eggs are, place them in a bowl of cold water. Eggs develop air pockets as they age, so an egg that is fresh will sink to the bottom of the bowl.

egg noodles   While no other product contains the same formulation, you can substitute myriad eggless pastas. You can use any small shape macaroni or small shells, or for the effect of the ribbons, break strands of pappardelle into shorter lengths. When using pasta, cook it longer than al dente because cooked egg noodles are suppler than pasta.

egg roll wrappers   Egg roll wrappers are thin sheets of pasta dough made with wheat flour and sometimes eggs. They're sold fresh, usually in the produce department. Rice paper pancakes, traditionally used for crispier spring rolls, are shelf-stable and the best substitution. You can also use flour tortillas, although they're thicker.

egg wash   Brushing baked goods with an egg wash, or egg that's been beaten with a bit of milk, before baking makes them brown and shiny. The same can be accomplished by brushing the unbaked items with water and then sprinkling them with granulated sugar.

eggnog   It wouldn't be the holidays without a carton in the house. For a substitute, soften vanilla ice cream and add nutmeg and liquor to it.

eggplant   Eggplant has a meatiness, even if it's cooked very soft. Portobello mushroom caps capture the same meatiness; the flavor of zucchini makes it a good substitute as well.

Eiswein (*ICE-vine*)   See wine, dessert.

elderberry   These tart, almost black-purple berries make delicious pies and jams. Either cranberries or sour cherries cook at the same rate.

elk   *See* game meat.

Emmenthaler (*em-en-TALL-er*)   See cheese.

endive   See lettuce.

English muffin   What distinguishes these yeast-risen flat cakes cooked on a griddle is the interior airy structure, which is why they're split before toasting. Crumpets, an English specialty, have a similar structure. You can also substitute a thick slice or two of toast.

enoki mushroom (*en-oh-key*)   See mushroom, wild.

epazote (*ep-ah-ZOOT-eh*)   This strongly flavored herb is used in many traditional Mexican dishes. It's hard to find it fresh even in Hispanic markets, but it's easy to find dried. You can use half fresh marjoram and half fresh cilantro as a substitute.

escargot (*ess-car-goh*)   See snails.

escarole (*ES-car-roll*)   See lettuce.

espresso   The favorite Italian drink is a method more than an ingredient; steam is forced through dark roasted coffee. You can duplicate the flavor with brewed coffee using twice the amount of coffee as you would for a regular cup. Use instant espresso powder and water as directed on the package.

evaporated milk   The volume of evaporated milk is half that of whole milk before it's sterilized. To substitute, boil whole milk until its volume is reduced by half. Or if there's other liquid, such as stock, in a recipe, use whole milk and decrease the amount of other liquid to compensate. *See also* milk.

Explorateur (*ex-plor-ah-tour*)   *See* cheese.

falafel (*fah-LA-fell*)   Based on garbanzo beans, falafel are the french fries of the Middle East, and they're often served with a sesame tahini sauce. To substitute, you could fry patties made from canned refried beans.

farfalle (*far-FAH-lay*)   *See* pasta, dried.

farfel (*FAR-fell*)   Farfel is always tiny bits of carbohydrate, but its nature can change. It can be tiny pasta cooked in soup, and such shapes as orzo or acini de peppe are good substitutions. However, in Jewish cooking, farfel is usually a side dish made with bits of broken noodles. In that case, crushed matzo or crackers are your best choices.

farina   This almost flavorless coarse flour is cooked as a breakfast cereal. Both semolina and cornmeal can be successfully used in its place.

farmer's cheese   This is actually a form of cottage cheese from which most of the liquid has been removed. Make it yourself by placing cottage cheese in a sieve over a mixing bowl. Allow it to drain, refrigerated, for 3 hours. Ricotta cheese can be used in place of farmer's cheese, but it may add more liquid to a recipe.

fatback   *See* bacon.

fats and oils   These categories are an essential part of cooking, although they should be used in moderation. Fats are a cooking medium that lubricate food and transfer heat from the pan to the food being cooked. Fats can reach a far higher temperature than water, so it's possible not only to cook foods faster in fats, but also to achieve the crispy exterior surface we associate with fried foods. As an ingredient, fats smooth and moisten the textures of many foods, as well as allowing for the transference of flavor. In most baked goods, fat plays an essential role in the development of the physical structure.

Saturation of fats refers to the structure of the particular fatty acid. Hydrogen atoms are held by the carbon atoms in the fatty acid structure. If no hydrogen atoms are missing, the fat is considered *saturated*. If one pair is missing, it is a *monounsaturated fat*. When two or more pairs of hydrogen atoms are missing, it's referred to as a *polyunsaturated fat*. Many polyunsaturated fats can contain *trans fat* and should be avoided.

Sub-Text

Trans fat is formed when liquid oils undergo a process called hydrogenation to make them more solid, as in the production of vegetable shortening and stick margarine. Processed foods such as cookies and snack foods are made with trans fat because it allows for a longer shelf life. Conclusive evidence now shows that trans fat raises the LDL (bad) cholesterol and lowers the HDL (good) cholesterol, which can clog arteries.

Predominant Fat Types

Saturated	Monounsaturated	Polyunsaturated
Animal fat	avocado oil	canola oil
Butter	olive oil	corn oil

continues

Predominant Fat Types   (continued)

Saturated	Monounsaturated	Polyunsaturated
Coconut oil	peanut oil	cottonseed oil
Cream	soybean oil	safflower oil
Lard	stick margarines*	sesame oil
Palm oil	sunflower oil	
	tub margarines	
	vegetable shortening*	

* Contains trans fat.

For cooking, you can substitute any of the bland vegetable oils for another, as they have a similar high smoke point. Canola, corn, peanut, sesame, and safflower oils all have relatively high smoke points of 440°F. Olive oil and lard tend to smoke at 375°F, while butter and margarine, unless they have been clarified, burn at much lower temperatures.

For baking, butter and margarine can be used interchangeably. If using vegetable shortening or lard, both of which are 100 percent fat, add 1 tablespoon liquid per cup of shortening.

fava beans (*FAH-vah*)   Fresh lima beans are the best substitute for fava beans, and they're also easier to cook because they don't require blanching to remove the tough skins before they're cooked. Edamame and garbanzo beans are also good choices.

feijoa (*fay-JO-ah*)   This aromatic tropical fruit has cream-colored flesh that tastes like a cross between grapes and pineapple. A mixture of those two fruits, or kiwifruit, is the best stand-in.

fennel   Sometimes called *anise* or *sweet anise* in markets, fennel has a texture like that of celery but with a light licorice flavor. If eating it raw, use celery instead and add a bit of anise seed to a salad dressing. If enjoying it cooked, braise either Belgian endive or celery in place of fennel, and add a drop or two of Pernod or another anise-flavored liqueur to the braising liquid.

fennel seed   Fennel seed—light brown and elliptical—is what gives Italian sausage its characteristic flavor, and it's used in many dishes to impart a slight licorice undertone. Anise seed can be used as a direct substitute in the same quantity.

fenugreek While these brown seeds that combine both bitter and sweet flavors are not common in most European cuisines, they are used as an ingredient in curry powder.

1 TB. fenugreek seeds, ground = 2 tsp. brown mustard seeds + 1 tsp. celery seeds, ground

fermented black beans Used in Chinese cooking to flavor sauces, these tiny black soybeans are preserved in salt so their flavor is both pungent and salty. There's no perfect substitute, but 3 tablespoons soy sauce for each 1 tablespoon fermented black beans adds the same level of salt.

feta (*FEH-tah*) *See* cheese.

fettuccine (*feh-too-CHEE-neh*) *See* pasta, dried.

fiddlehead fern A harbinger of spring, fiddlehead ferns are the tightly coiled shoots from ostrich ferns. Their flavor is like a cross between asparagus and green beans, so very thin asparagus or French haricot verts are your best choices.

figs, dried These vary greatly, depending on which of the many species of figs grown around the world were dried. For both a similar flavor and size, use pitted dried dates. If the figs were to be chopped finely, try raisins or dried currants.

figs, fresh It's only been in the last decade that Americans other than those in sunny California have had access to luscious fresh figs with their soft purple interior dotted with seeds. Ripe plums, especially tiny Italian prune plums available in the fall, are the best substitute.

filbert *See* hazelnut.

filé powder (*fee-lay*) The leaves from the sassafras tree native to Louisiana are ground into a powder, sometimes called filé gumbo. It's used to thicken gumbo and other dishes as an alternative to okra, which is the best substitution.

1 TB. filé powder = 1 lb. sliced okra or 1 TB. cornstarch mixed with 2 TB. cold water

filet mignon *See* beef.

filo   *See* phyllo.

fines herbs (*feen erb*)   Used both fresh and dried, fines herbs is a mixture of equal parts parsley, tarragon, chervil, and chives. You can find it dried in the spice aisle, but it's even better if you make it fresh yourself.

finnan haddie   Smoking fish as a means of preservation is part of every cuisine, and this popular dish is Scottish haddock that's been smoked. With its flavor and texture, smoked bluefish or smoked mackerel are your best options. *See also* cod.

fish sauce   Used in Thai, Vietnamese, Japanese, and Philippine cooking, this pungent and salty sauce is made by fermenting anchovies and other fish parts.

¼ cup fish sauce = 3 TB. soy sauce + 1 TB. anchovy paste

flageolet (*flah-joh-lay*)   *See* beans, dried.

flank steak   *See* beef.

flanken   *See* beef.

flounder   A member of the flatfish family, flounder swims in many waters around the world, and sole is your best alternative.

flour   Flour is made from wheat, but that's where the similarities end, and the function of the flour in a recipe determines what you can use in its place. Flour is used as an essential ingredient to create the structure in baked goods, and it's also used as a coating for foods to be cooked and as a thickening agent for sauces.

For baking: One constant is the volume; 1 pound flour equals 3½ cups (unsifted), with the exception of cake flour, which is 4 cups. What makes each flour different is its protein content, which effects its ability to absorb liquid. Hard wheat grown in northern climates is more absorbent than soft wheat grown in the south, and its gluten content is higher. For foods like cakes, you want very low gluten content to keep the cake tender, but for bread, you need a flour with a much higher gluten content to allow the dough to expand as it rises.

all-purpose   This flour comes both bleached and unbleached; they can be used interchangeably.

1 cup all-purpose flour = 1 cup + 3 TB. cake flour

bread This flour is made almost exclusively with hard wheat that has a small amount of malt barley added to boost yeast production and a bit of vitamin C to make the resulting dough more elastic.

1 cup bread flour = 1 cup all-purpose flour + 1 TB. gluten flour

cake This flour is milled to a finer texture and contains a large percentage of soft wheat.

1 cup cake flour = ⅞ cup all-purpose flour sifted with 2 TB. cornstarch

Sub-Text

Sifting is the process of passing flour and sometimes other ingredients through a wire mesh strainer. Sifting lightens the flour and adds volume, as well as ridding it of any lumps. Flour is frequently sifted with other dry ingredients to create a homogeneous mix.

pastry This has more gluten than cake flour but not as much as all-purpose, which is why it's recommended for cookies and biscuits.

1 cup pastry flour = ⅔ cup all-purpose flour + ⅓ cup cake flour

self-rising This was introduced as a convenience to make cake batters without measuring additional ingredients.

1 cup self-rising flour = 1 cup cake flour + ½ tsp. baking powder + ¼ tsp. salt

whole wheat While whole-wheat flour is excellent for the diet because of the additional vitamins, minerals, and bran it contains, it also has considerably more gluten and should not be used exclusively for baked goods.

1 cup whole-wheat flour = ⅞ cup all-purpose flour + 2 TB. wheat germ

For thickening: Flour adds viscosity to a sauce in a few ways, but what's important is to coat the flour particles with grease in some way to eliminate a pasty taste. If food is coated in flour before browning, the fat in the pan serves that purpose; otherwise, the flour is cooked with butter or oil before adding it to liquid.

2 TB. all-purpose flour = 1 TB. cornstarch, arrowroot, or potato starch mixed with 2 TB. cold water

For cooking: Some foods are coated with flour before being dipped into an egg wash and crumbs or into a batter. The flour creates a glue to keep the batter attached. For this purpose, cornstarch or potato starch can be used.

fluke   A member of the flatfish family, any flounder, sole, or European turbot can be substituted successfully and has the same texture and flavor.

flying fish roe   *See* caviar.

focaccia (*foh-CAH-che-yah*)   This fairly flat Italian bread brushed with olive oil, salt, and many times herbs or olives before baking is gaining in popularity. If your supermarket offers balls of refrigerated bread or pizza dough, you can make it yourself, or buy a loaf of Italian bread and cut it in half horizontally. Then treat the cut surfaces with olive oil and herbs.

foie gras (*fwah grah*)   In French, this literally means "fat liver," and while the animal in question in France is usually a goose, in the United States, it's a moulard duck. If cooking it as part of a mousse or terrine, substitute duck livers, which will be more gamey in flavor, at the proportion of 50 percent duck liver and 50 percent unsalted butter. Calves' liver is the best alternative for sautéed foie gras; cook it quickly to keep it rare.

fontina (*fon-TEE-nah*)   *See* cheese.

fortified wine   *See* wine, fortified.

fowl   *See* chicken.

fraise des bois (*fraiz day bwah*)   These tiny French strawberries are the sweetest and most succulent you'll ever eat. While conventional strawberries pale by comparison, they remain the best substitution choice.

Framboise (*fram-boize*)   *See* brandy, fruit.

Frangelico (*fran-GEL-i-coh*)   *See* liqueur.

French dressing   French dressing is typically a simple vinaigrette flavored with herbs, shallots, and Dijon mustard. Any vinaigrette can be used in its place, or you can make it easily yourself.

Yield: ½ cup

3 TB. white or red wine vinegar	½ tsp. dried thyme
1 TB. finely chopped shallot	Salt and freshly ground black pepper
2 tsp. Dijon mustard	⅓ cup olive oil

Combine vinegar, shallot, Dijon mustard, thyme, salt, and pepper in a jar with a tight-fitting lid, and shake well. Add olive oil, and shake well again. Refrigerate dressing for up to a week, tightly covered.

Fresco chili   *See* chilies, fresh.

friar plum   *See* plums.

frisée (*free-say*)   *See* lettuce.

frogs' legs   The flavor of frogs' hind legs has been compared to very tender and only slightly fishy chicken. Chicken breast can always be used in its place, as can bay scallops.

fromage blanc (*froh-magh blahnk*)   In France, this soft fresh cheese is eaten as dessert, topped with fruit and a sauce. Mixing equal parts of cream cheese and heavy cream gives you a similar flavor and texture.

fudge   The creamy texture and over-the-top sweet flavor is what defines fudge, which can be made from chocolate, with maple syrup, or many flavors. For chocolate, a ganache is similar.

Fumé Blanc (*foo-may blahn*)   *See* wine, white.

fusilli (*foo-SEE-lee*)   *See* pasta, dried.

G

galangal (*goo-LANG-guhl*)   Sometimes called Thai ginger, this rhizome has a flavor similar to ginger but with more pepper.

1 TB. grated fresh galangal = 1 TB. grated fresh ginger + ½ tsp. freshly ground black pepper

Galliano (*gal-lee-YAH-noh*)   *See* liqueur.

game bird   It's increasingly more common to find game birds in supermarkets. Most are farm-raised, so they're handled in a manner similar to chicken. They don't have the "gamey" flavor of their wild cousins, nor are they hung to age and tenderize their flesh. But their meat still has far more flavor and texture than even a free-range chicken, and their small size means that presentations can be dramatic for individual diners.

guinea hen   These birds come in a wide range of sizes, from less than 1 pound to about 3 pounds. Females (hens) are preferred to the males, because the hens are more tender.

partridge   Partridges are usually about 1 pound. Look for young, tender birds because older partridge is often tough. These birds have an excellent flavor but are not as delicate as squab or pheasant.

pheasant   Generally pheasant is sold at 2 to 2½ pounds, but young pheasants of 1 pound or less are also available. They have delicate, light-colored meat with subtle flavor. Pheasant must be handled carefully because it can be very dry if overcooked.

quail   The small quail usually weighs 4 to 5 ounces, so a normal portion is 2 birds, unless they're stuffed. Perhaps the most popular and widely available of the small birds, quail are richly flavored without a strong taste. They have meaty breasts for their size, but there's not much meat on their legs.

Toque Tips

When grilling quail, hold them flat by inserting bamboo skewers through them in an X pattern. Remove the skewers before serving, or serve them with the skewers for something different.

squab   Squab can weigh from 12 to 20 ounces, and the smaller ones are generally more tender. Squab is widely available and favored for its moist, meaty dark flesh with a faintly gamey flavor. Squab is often considered the best all-purpose game bird.

You can find game birds in supermarkets, but it might be difficult to find all varieties. The following table offers some substitutions when you can't find what you're looking for.

Game Birds at a Glance

Bird	Flesh Color	Flavor	Substitution
Guinea hen	light/medium	earthy/sweet	pheasant
Partridge	light pink	woodsy, earthy	squab
Pheasant	light/medium	chicken	quail
Quail	light/medium	poussin	pheasant
Squab	dark	mildly gamey	partridge

game hen   *See* chicken.

game meat   Long available but not greatly appreciated, game meats are gaining popularity as people seek lower fat and more flavor in their foods. Game meats are lower in cholesterol than other meats, and when handled properly, they are tender with intriguing flavors. The following table offers a summary of what's on the market and what you can substitute.

Game Meats at a Glance

Meat	Flavor	Substitution
Antelope	stronger than venison	venison
Boar	strong-tasting pork	pork
Buffalo	delicate and lean	beef
Elk	form of venison	venison or beef
Moose	form of venison	venison or beef
Ostrich	very much like steak	beef
Reindeer	form of venison	venison or beef
Venison	like gamey beef	antelope or beef

Toque Tips

All game meats can benefit from a day in a red wine marinade to break down the fibers and make the meat more tender, whether it's to be quickly grilled or slowly braised.

ganache (*gan-aahsh*)   This rich mixture of chocolate, butter, and cream is used as an easy glaze or frosting for cakes, or it can be chilled, rolled into balls, and dusted with cocoa powder for truffles.

Yield: 1 cup

6 oz. chopped bittersweet
  chocolate

6 TB. unsalted butter
3 TB. heavy cream

Combine chocolate with butter and heavy cream in a small saucepan. Heat over low heat, stirring occasionally, until mixture is melted and glossy.

garam masala (*GHA-ram MAH-sa-lah*)   *See* curry powder.

garbanzo bean (*gar-BAHN-zoh*) (or **chick pea**) *See* beans, dried.

garlic This aromatic member of the lily family is a first cousin to shallots, and those are the best substitute. You can find granulated garlic and garlic powder, but their flavor is very harsh and chemical compared to fresh garlic.

1 garlic clove, peeled and minced = 1 tsp.

1 tsp. minced fresh garlic = 1 TB. minced shallot, ¼ tsp. granulated garlic, or ⅛ tsp. garlic powder

garlic chives Garlic chives look like chives, but have a decidedly garlic aftertaste.

¼ cup chopped garlic chives = ¼ cup chopped chives + 2 garlic cloves, peeled and minced, or ¼ cup chopped green scallion tops + 2 garlic cloves, peeled and minced

garlic salt This convenient seasoning is a mixture of table salt and garlic powder.

1 tsp. garlic salt = ¾ tsp. salt + ¼ tsp. garlic powder or ¾ tsp. salt + 1 garlic clove, peeled and minced

gelatin A pure protein that comes from beef and veal bones and other parts of animals, it takes 1 tablespoon granulated gelatin to jell 2 cups liquid.

1 TB. granulated gelatin = 4 gelatin sheets or 2 tsp. agar (suitable for vegetarians)

 **Food Foibles**

Soak gelatin in a cold liquid for 3 to 5 minutes to soften it before dissolving it in hot liquid. Otherwise, the gelatin will remain granular.

gemelli (*gem-ELLY*) *See* pasta, dried.

Gewürztraminer (*guh-VURTS-tra-meen-er*) *See* wine, white.

ghee *See* butter, clarified.

gherkin   These tiny cucumbers are raised to become pickles, and it's almost impossible to find them fresh except at summer farmers' markets. For gherkin pickles, French chornichon are almost identical in flavor. If you want to make tiny pickles yourself, cut English cucumbers into pieces 2 inches long and ½ inch wide.

gin   *See* spirits.

ginger   A tropical rhizome, ginger is an essential ingredient in Asian cooking; its taste is somewhat sweet and partially hot with a distinctive aroma. Fresh and ground ginger have similar flavors, but the dried version does not provide the same seductive aroma.

1 TB. grated fresh ginger = ¼ tsp. ground ginger or 2 TB. crystallized ginger, rinsed to remove the sugar and finely chopped

ginger, crystallized   Used primarily for desserts, this is ginger that's been simmered in a sugar syrup, which both tenderizes and sweetens it. It's then dusted with granulated sugar to keep the slices from sticking together. You can substitute 1 tablespoon grated fresh ginger and 2 tablespoons granulated sugar for each 3 tablespoons crystallized ginger.

ginger, pickled   Used most often as a garnish for Japanese dishes like sushi, this ginger has been preserved in sweet rice vinegar. Spicy cucumber pickle slices are the best substitute.

gingersnaps   Flavored with molasses, these spicy cookies contain ground ginger. German pfeffernüesse are almost identical in flavor and texture. Gingersnaps are frequently used in place of graham crackers for a crumb crust. In that case, substitute graham cracker or vanilla wafer crumbs, and add ½ teaspoon ground ginger per 1 cup crumbs. If a recipe calls for sugar to be added to the mixture, substitute dark brown sugar for granulated sugar.

girolle (*gheer-ool*)   *See* mushroom, wild.

glace de viande (*glahs duh vee-yand*)   In French cooking, this thick paste is used to add color and flavor to meat dishes. To substitute, add a 1-ounce package brown gravy mix in place of 1 tablespoon glace de viande. Or make it yourself.

Yield: ½ *cup*

1 qt. salt-free beef or veal stock

Remove all fat from stock, and bring it to a boil over medium-high heat. Reduce the heat to medium, and cook liquid until only ½ cup remains.

glass noodles   *See* cellophane noodles.

Gloucester cheese   *See* cheese.

gnocchi (*KNOW-key*)   These tiny boiled Italian dumplings are most frequently made with potato, although they can also be made with flour or farina. You can probably find frozen gnocchi in your local supermarket. Thick egg noodles or German spaetzle are the best substitutes.

goat cheese   *See* cheese.

goose   A goose feeds about 6 people; duck meat is almost identical in flavor but smaller and feeds about 4. Turkey or chicken thighs are good substitutes, but don't substitute white meat poultry for this dark meat bird.

Gorgonzola (*gor-gon-ZOH-la*)   *See* cheese.

Gouda (*GOO-dah*)   *See* cheese.

graham cracker   These rectangular whole-wheat crackers traditionally sweetened with honey were invented as a healthy snack in the early nineteenth century. English whole-wheat cheese biscuits have a similar color and flavor; for a crust, you can use crushed gingersnaps or vanilla wafers.

Grand Marnier (*gran marn-yay*)   *See* liqueur, orange.

granola   This breakfast cereal can be made with myriad ingredients, but it almost always includes oats, nuts, and dried fruit. Muesli has an almost identical formulation and frequently less fat.

granulated sugar   *See* sugar.

grape   Genetic engineering has produced the seedless grape, which is easy to find year-round. If color is not a concern, green, red, and purple grapes can be substituted for each other randomly. If green color is important, use small balls of honeydew melon; if red color is needed, cut plums into grape-size pieces.

grape leaf   In Greek and Middle Eastern cooking, grape leaves are used for wrapping food, and unless you spot some vines on the side of the road, chances are you'll buy them brined in jars. The best alternatives are small Savoy cabbage leaves or Swiss chard. If using Savoy cabbage, blanch them in boiling water for 5 minutes; if using Swiss chard, remove the large center rib and blanch for 3 minutes.

grapefruit   This tart member of the citrus family, native to the New World, has a unique taste. The closest in flavor is ugli fruit. Orange segments, sprinkled with lemon or lime juice, are another alternative.

grappa   *See* brandy.

gravlax (*GRAHV-locks*)   This Swedish specialty is actually raw salmon that's been cured with salt, sugar, and herbs, and weighted for a few days. Smoked salmon has a similar flavor and richness.

Great Northern bean   *See* beans, dried.

green bean   Also dubbed *string beans* because of the fibrous "string" running down its back, green beans are edible pods that contain small seeds. A yellow version is called a wax bean, and tiny thin green beans are marketed by their French name, *haricot verts*. If neither option is available, sugar snap peas or snow peas are good alternatives, as are very thin asparagus spears, although asparagus has a more assertive flavor.

green onion   *See* scallion.

green pepper   *See* bell pepper.

green peppercorn   *See* peppercorn.

Greengage plum   *See* plum.

greens   The term *greens* is used for numerous leafy green vegetables with a spicy bite and sometimes a bitter flavor. They come in other colors besides green, and some are fine as salad inclusions, too. They're all too strong to eat raw alone, but you can toss a small portion with your lettuces.

broccoli rabe (or ***rapini***)   This is a variety of broccoli cultivated for its leaf and stem growth and has a more pungent flavor than standard broccoli flowers. It's best kept crisp-tender after cooking.

collards   This medium-green leaf is one of the mildest greens, with a flavor between that of cabbage and kale. The leaf edges have a torn appearance.

dandelion greens   These do not come from the same plant as the common dandelion, although the long, slender, pale green pointed leaves with toothed edges look the same. They have a slightly bitter flavor and can be used in a salad similar to watercress.

kale   Botanically a member of the cabbage family, the leaves of kale are long and substantial, with a musty-green to blue-green color and curled edges. The flavor is mild, and a small portion can be used raw in salads.

mustard greens   These large, oval green leaves with frilly edges are greens with a spunky, pungent, and bitter flavor similar to mustard. Very young mustard greens are excellent raw in a salad, while older greens can have quite a bitter taste, which is best tempered with cooking.

Swiss chard   Swiss chard is actually a variety of beet that does not develop a tuberous root. It has floppy, dark green leaves with purple or white veins and stalks. The stems taste very mild similar to celery, and the leaves are a mild flavor similar to spinach but earthier. Swiss chard can be used both raw and cooked.

turnip greens   Turnip greens are long sleek leaves that have a wonderful, assertively bitter flavor. The texture remains firm and chewy, even when thoroughly cooked.

Some greens are delightful if quickly cooked, and others really need to be simmered for a long time. Traditional cooks simmered greens for hours, until they were virtually falling apart. The cooking range given in the following table gives you latitude depending on the texture you prefer for cooked greens.

Greens at a Glance

Green	Cooking Technique(s)	Cook Time
Broccoli rabe	sauté, steam, simmer	2 to 6 min.
Collards	simmer	20 min. to 2 hr.
Dandelion	stir-fry	3 to 5 min.
Kale	sauté, steam, stir-fry	5 to 25 min.
Mustard greens	simmer	10 to 30 min.
Swiss chard	sauté, steam, stir-fry	stems: 10 min. leaves: 2 min.
Turnip greens	simmer	20 to 40 min.

Grenache (*gren-ash*)   *See* wine, red.

grenadine   Authentic grenadine is heavily sweetened pomegranate juice, so pomegranate juice concentrate is your best alternative. Raspberry syrup or red currant syrup are options, or if all else fails, thin raspberry or red currant jelly with water at the ratio of 50 percent each.

grits   *See* cornmeal.

groat   *See* buckwheat groat.

grouper   This fish found in the warm waters of the Gulf of Mexico and the southern Atlantic is a member of the sea bass family, so any sea bass shares its delicate flavor and firm texture. Other options are red snapper, redfish, and halibut.

Gruyère (*gree-yahr*)   *See* cheese.

guacamole (*wok-ah-MOH-lay*)   This classic of all Mexican dips is easy to make at home; the key to success is to use ripe avocados.

Yield: 3 cups

5 ripe avocados

1 small red onion, peeled and finely diced

1 or 2 jalapeño chilies, seeds and ribs removed, and finely diced

½ cup chopped fresh cilantro

3 TB. freshly squeezed lime juice

Salt

Place avocado in a bowl with red onion and chilies and mash mixture together with a fork, leaving some avocado in chunks. Add cilantro and lime juice, and season with salt. Mix well. You can make guacamole up to 8 hours in advance; push a piece of plastic wrap directly into the surface, and refrigerate.

G

guava (*GUA-vah*)   This tropical fruit boasts both sweet and sour flavors, and its flesh can range from bright yellow to bright red, depending on the species. Both pineapple and raspberries are good alternatives.

guero (*GWEH-roh*)   *See* chilies, fresh.

guinea hen   *See* game bird.

habañero chili (*ha-bahn-YHER-oh*)   *See* chilies, fresh.

haddock   *See* cod.

hake   *See* cod.

half-and-half   *See* cream.

halibut   Most abundant in the spring and summer in cold waters, this firm-fleshed flatfish is prized for its mild flavor. Any of the cod species, turbot, or striped bass can be used in its place.

ham   There are literally hundreds of hams around the world, and the only common denominator is that they all start out as fresh pork from a hog's upper hind leg. If hams are large, they're usually divided into shank and butt ends. The butt end is meatier but contains more fat; the shank end contains only one bone so it's easier to carve. Most of the hams in markets are basic "city hams"—the generic American ham. But you'll see many fancy hams listed in recipes, so here's a guide to them.

Ham at a Glance

Ham	Origin	Description	Substitution
American	USA	brine-cured	Canadian bacon
Ardennes	France	air-dried	prosciutto
Bayonne	France	air-dried	prosciutto
Black Forest	Germany	smoked with pine, black exterior	Virginia

Ham	Origin	Description	Substitution
Country	USA	air-dried and smoked	prosciutto
Prosciutto	Italy	air-dried, served raw	Smithfield
Serrano	Spain	dry-cured, served raw	prosciutto
Smithfield	USA	air-dried and smoked	country
Tasso	USA	highly spiced and smoked	Canadian bacon
Virginia	USA	brine-cured	any American
Westphalian	Germany	salty and smoked with juniper	Black Forest

ham hock This cured and smoked lower joint of a pig's back leg is used for seasoning soups, stews, and other hearty dishes; it usually weighs about 1 pound. Smoked pig gowls are the closest substitute in the low-priced category, and although it's more expensive, you can use a ½-pound chunk of smoked ham. Another alternative is to use a smoked turkey drumstick or smoked turkey wings, both of which are readily accessible in supermarkets.

hamburger *See* beef, ground.

hard sauce A rich mixture of butter, confectioners' sugar, and some sort of flavoring, hard sauce is used as a topping for traditional steamed puddings, and it can also be used for bread pudding or any homey and hot dessert. Any butter-based icing can be substituted.

Yield: 1½ cups

4 cups (1 lb.) confectioners' sugar

¼ lb. unsalted butter, cut into 10 pieces and softened

2 TB. brandy, rum, or bourbon, or 2 TB. water mixed with ¼ tsp. extract

Combine sugar and butter in a food processor fitted with a steel blade. Process until well combined. Add liquid, and process until light and fluffy, scraping the sides of the work bowl as necessary. Hard sauce can be refrigerated for up to 1 week, tightly covered.

hare   *See* rabbit.

haricot verts (*har-e-coh vehr*)   *See* green bean.

harissa (*har-EE-sah*)   Found in the Middle Eastern section of super-markets, harissa is a fiery paste made from red chilies, spices, and garlic used in Moroccan cooking.

> *1 TB. harissa = 2 tsp. Chinese chili paste with garlic + 2 garlic cloves, peeled and minced + ½ tsp. ground cumin; 1½ tsp. cayenne; or 2 tsp. hot red pepper sauce*

Havarti (*hah-VAHR-tee*)   *See* cheese.

hazelnut   Frequently called filberts, hazelnuts are one of the most buttery and aromatic nuts. For baking, macadamia nuts and almonds are the best alternatives and can be used in the same volume. For cooking, hazelnut oil delivers the flavor; use 2 tablespoons per 1 cup hazelnuts. The dish won't have the thick texture provided by ground nuts, though.

hearts of palm   Only in the past few years have fresh hearts of palm shown up in specialty markets; most of us grew up with the canned versions. They have a crispy texture if fresh and their flavor is grassy with hints of asparagus or artichoke. Cooked white asparagus, your best bet, shares both color and shape. In a salad, try artichoke hearts.

Toque Tips

Most recipes call for hazelnuts to be peeled, which is how you'll find them most of the time. If you have to peel them yourself, it's easy: bake the nuts in a 350°F oven for 10 to 12 minutes or until you see the skins begin to split. Roll the nuts around in a cloth tea towel, and the skins will rub right off.

heavy cream   *See* cream.

herbes de Provence (*erb duh pro-vawz*)   Found in the spice section of many supermarkets and gourmet stores, this dried blend of many herbs is associated with the sunny cuisine of Provence, in the south of France. To make it yourself, combine equal parts dried basil, thyme, fennel, rosemary, sage, lavender, crushed fennel seed, and marjoram.

Herbsaint   *See* liqueur.

herring   These tiny fish can be smoked, cured, pickled, or some combination of all three. Canned sardines are a good substitute for mild-
flavored herring, as are English kippers. For smoked herring, try smoked
whitefish or smoked trout as an alternative; they will be the same color
and similar in flavor.

hickory nut   These native American nuts are difficult to find and
almost never sold already shelled. Pecans are a member of the same
family, and their taste is almost identical.

hoisin sauce (*hoy-ZAHN*)   Used both as a condiment and an ingredient, hoisin sauce is the ketchup of Chinese cooking. This thick, sweet
and spicy reddish-brown sauce is a mixture of soybeans, garlic, chilies,
Chinese five-spice powder, and sugar.

> *$1/2$ cup hoisin sauce = $1/4$ cup ketchup + 2 TB. molasses + 1 TB. soy sauce +
> 1 tsp. Chinese five-spice powder*

hollandaise sauce (*holl-uhn-dayz*)   A classic of the French repertoire,
hollandaise is an emulsion of egg yolks and butter seasoned with a bit of
lemon juice. Although it won't be as rich, a white sauce can be used in its
place for hot dishes, and a mayonnaise sauce can be used for cold foods.

hominy   *See* cornmeal.

honey   Although the floral accents from this sweet nectar made by
bees cannot be duplicated, you can add liquid sweetness to recipes. Try
light or dark corn syrup and maple syrup in direct quantities, or combine
1 cup granulated or light brown sugar with $1/4$ cup liquid from the recipe
and stir well to dissolve the sugar.

honeydew melon   *See* melon.

horseradish   The acrid fumes from grating spicy and pungent fresh
horseradish root can be downright painful—and is probably why most
of us purchase prepared horseradish, which has vinegar and salt added.
Fresh horseradish is twice as strong as prepared, so only use half the
amount. Wasabi is a Japanese form of horseradish that's available both
as a powder and a paste. Use 1 teaspoon wasabi for each 1 tablespoon
prepared horseradish.

hot cherry pepper   *See* chilies, fresh.

hot red pepper sauce   Tabasco might have invented this genre of cayenne peppers mellowed in salted vinegar, but today you can find shelves full of hot red pepper sauces. Substitute ⅛ teaspoon cayenne or ¼ teaspoon crushed red pepper flakes for each ½ teaspoon hot red pepper sauce.

hubbard squash   The hubbard is one of the largest members of the winter squash family. Its flesh isn't as creamy as that of acorn or butternut squash, but those can be substituted on a direct basis, as can fresh or canned pumpkin.

huckleberry   The main difference between the blue-black huckleberry and a blueberry is the seeds. The seeds of a blueberry are soft, while those of a huckleberry, which is its wild cousin, are hard. Blueberries can be used interchangeably in any recipe.

hummus (*HUM-muss*)   This Middle Eastern dip stars garbanzo beans and tahini, a sesame seed paste. It's readily available in the refrigerated case at supermarkets, but it's also easy to make it yourself.

Yield: 2 cups

1 (15-oz.) can garbanzo
  beans, drained and rinsed
2 garlic cloves, peeled
¼ cup tahini, well stirred
2 or 3 TB. freshly squeezed
  lemon juice

¼ cup olive oil
2 TB. chopped fresh parsley
Salt and freshly ground black
  pepper

Combine garbanzo beans, garlic, tahini, lemon juice, and olive oil in a food processor fitted with a steel blade and purée until smooth. Scrape mixture into a bowl, stir in parsley, and season with salt and pepper. Hummus can be refrigerated for up to a week, tightly covered.

Food Foibles

Tahini is made from ground sesame seeds, which contain a large amount of sesame oil. That oil always rises to the top, so it's important to stir it well before measuring it.

ice cream   Light ice cream and frozen yogurt both contain less fat, and a similar product based on tofu contains no dairy products.

ice wine   *See* wine, dessert.

iceberg lettuce   *See* lettuce.

infused oil   *See* oil, infused.

Irish whiskey   *See* spirits.

Italian bread   What usually differentiates Italian bread from French is the shape; Italian bread is wider and is frequently topped with sesame seeds. Any crusty loaf of French bread or a baguette can be substituted. If the slices of Italian bread need to be wide for sandwiches, slice the French bread on the diagonal.

Italian dressing   Italian seasonings like basil and oregano along with garlic characterize this version of vinaigrette. Any vinegar-based dressing can be used in its place, or you can make it easily yourself.

Yield: ½ cup

3 TB. white or red wine
   vinegar
1 TB. chopped fresh parsley
2 garlic cloves, peeled and
   minced

1 tsp. dried oregano
½ tsp. dried basil
Salt and freshly ground black
   pepper
⅓ cup olive oil

---

continues

continued

> Combine vinegar, parsley, garlic, oregano, basil, salt, and pepper in a jar with a tight-fitting lid, and shake well. Add olive oil, and shake well again. Dressing can be refrigerated for up to a week, tightly covered.

Italian eggplant   Italian eggplants look like the small children of traditional eggplants; they're the same shape and color but about ⅓ the size.

3 Italian eggplants = 1 common eggplant or 5 Japanese eggplants

Toque Tips

The seeds of Italian eggplants are very small and rarely bitter. If you're substituting a common eggplant, it's best to take the extra step of salting it to remove bitterness. Slice the eggplant and sprinkle the pieces liberally with salt. Place the slices in a colander and weight them with a plate topped with cans. Allow the slices to drain for 30 minutes, rinse, and squeeze them dry.

Italian meringue   What makes Italian meringue sturdy is that the sugar is boiled with a small amount of water and then added slowly to the egg whites. The American version of this is called boiled icing, or you can use any white buttercream frosting in its place.

Italian parsley   The Italian version of this ubiquitous herb has flat leaves, and most cooks believe it has a stronger and grassier flavor. But curly parsley can be substituted at any time. Cilantro can also be used, but it will add a musty and citrus flavor.

Italian sausage   Garlic and fennel are the distinguishing seasonings in Italian sausage, with crushed red pepper flakes added for the hot version. Use any pork sausage, add 1 tablespoon crushed fennel seeds per pound of meat, and adjust garlic according to personal preference.

Italian seasoning   This was one of the first preblended herb mixes on the market, and it's used not only in Italian but in most Mediterranean cooking as well. It's a mixture of basil, oregano, rosemary, and thyme, so any of these component ingredients can be substituted.

¼ cup Italian seasoning = 2 TB. dried oregano + 1 TB. dried basil + 1 tsp. dried thyme + 1 tsp. dried rosemary + 1 tsp. dried marjoram

jack cheese   *See* cheese.

jalapeño chili (*ha-lah-PAIN-yoh*)   *See* chilies, fresh.

jam   In the world of thickened fruit spreads, jam is in the middle. Preserves have larger pieces of fruit, and jelly has less or none. But the same amount and flavor of either preserves or jelly does the trick.

Jamaican jerk   Allspice and Scotch bonnet peppers, both indigenous to Jamaica, are the two key ingredients to this fiery flavoring that also includes other spices that's rubbed onto foods before grilling. Combine 2 tablespoons chili powder with 1 teaspoon thyme and ½ teaspoon allspice to approximate the flavor.

Japanese eggplant   Long, thin, and almost amethyst in color, Japanese eggplants are the most delicate of the species. They're the same length as Italian eggplants, but thinner.

5 Japanese eggplants = 3 Italian eggplants

Japanese horseradish *See* wasabi.

Japanese radish *See* daikon.

Jarlsberg (*YAHRLS-berg*) *See* cheese.

jasmine rice *See* rice.

jelly Jelly is most often made from reduced fruit juice rather than actual fruit, which is why it's clear; it's usually thickened by using pectin. Jam is thicker, and preserves contain even larger pieces of fruit than jam, but both can be substituted in equal amounts. If you want a smooth texture, purée the jam or preserves.

Jerusalem artichoke This vegetable is not related to the globe artichoke; it's a native American tuber that's a cousin of the sunflower and can be eaten raw or cooked. If you're eating them raw in a salad, celeriac, jicama, and kohlrabi are your best alternatives. If you're eating them cooked, celeriac, parsnips, or turnips have a similar color and flavor.

Food Foibles

Like apples, Jerusalem artichokes turn brown when exposed to air, so if you're eating them raw, toss them with the salad dressing immediately after slicing them to prevent discoloration.

jicama (*HEE-kim-ah*) This white-fleshed tuber coated with an inedible brown skin has the crunchiness of a water chestnut, with a slight hint of apple flavor. It's occasionally added to stir-fries, but most often eaten raw. Use either apples or water chestnuts instead. If using apples, toss them with lemon juice to prevent discoloration due to oxidation.

John Dory John Dory has a mild flavor and tender texture. Amongst the firm-fleshed whitefish, halibut, cod, grouper, and red snapper are the best alternatives.

juniper berries Juniper berries, the fruit of the evergreen juniper shrub, is what you taste when you sip gin, so gin is really the best substitute. Use ¼ cup gin for every 1 tablespoon juniper berries in a recipe and then subtract the gin from the liquid specified in the recipe.

junket Although it's fallen out of fashion, this milk-based pudding was very popular during the mid-twentieth century. Any cooked or instant pudding, either purchased or homemade, can be substituted.

kabocha squash (*kah-BOW-cha*) A newcomer to the winter squash family, a kabocha is about 3 pounds and has a vibrant green rind. Its sweet orange flesh is almost identical in color and flavor to either acorn or butternut squash.

kaffir lime (*ka-FIR*) This species of tropical lime is prized for its leaves, which add an herbaceous and citrus aroma and flavor to dishes. You'll find them dried most often, but you might get lucky and find some fresh in Asian markets.

3 kaffir lime leaves = 1 TB. grated lime zest

Kahlùa (*kah-LOO-ah*) *See* liqueur.

kalamata olive (*cal-ah-MAH-tah*) *See* olive.

kale *See* greens.

kasha (*kah-shah*) *See* buckwheat groat.

kasseri (*cah-SEHR-ee*) *See* cheese.

kefir (*KEY-fur*) This cultured milk beverage, found most often in health food stores, tastes very similar to yogurt.

1 cup kefir = ²/₃ cup plain yogurt + ¹/₃ cup milk

ketchup   This ubiquitous condiment has been around in some form for more than a century. For topping a burger, chili sauce is your best substitute because it has the same sweet-sour tomato profile, although it's not smooth. Or try your favorite barbecue sauce. In cooking, either of those choices work, too, or create the flavors in another way.

1 cup ketchup = ³/₄ cup tomato purée + 2 TB. granulated sugar + 1 TB. cider vinegar + ¹/₄ tsp. ground allspice

Key lime   Key limes are smaller than common limes, and their juice has a more concentrated and tart flavor. Key limes are becoming more common to find in the market, but the juice is available bottled and can be used in equal amounts.

¹/₄ cup Key lime juice = 3¹/₂ TB. freshly squeezed lime juice + 1¹/₂ tsp. freshly squeezed lemon juice

Toque Tips

You lose some aroma when you use a bottled citrus juice rather than a freshly squeezed one. Add ¹/₂ teaspoon grated zest to bottled juice—even if from a different citrus fruit—to improve the aroma.

kidney   Steak and kidney pie has been a mainstay of the English diet for centuries, but it has yet to gain popularity in the United States. Like all organ meats, kidneys are inherently tender because they're not comprised of muscle tissue. It's possible to find veal, beef, lamb, and pork kidneys on the market. For veal and lamb kidneys, sweetbreads are the best substitute because they're about the same size and have the same delicate texture. Use brains for beef or pork kidneys.

kidney bean   *See* beans, dried.

kielbasa (*keel-BAH-sah*)   Also sold as Polish sausage, kielbasa can be smoked or unsmoked and is always sold in links. Substitute any of the other smoked sausages, andouille, or linguiça.

While traditional kielbasa is made from pork, many turkey versions are available with lower cholesterol and fat content.

kimchee (*KIHM-chee*)   This fiery, hot pickled cabbage is served at every Korean meal. It's available fresh in many Asian markets or canned in supermarkets.

> *1 lb. kimchee = 1 lb. sauerkraut, drained, + 2 TB. adobo sauce or 1 TB. hot red pepper sauce*

kirsch, kirschwasser (*keersh, keersh-vaser*)   *See* brandy, fruit.

kiwi fruit   Officially called Chinese gooseberries, kiwi fruit became the darling of French nouvelle cuisine. The flavor of kiwi is like a cross between strawberry and melon with a tart citrus note. To top a pie or tart with the same green look, use halved green grapes drizzled with a bit of lime juice.

knockwurst (*knock-vurst*)   Part of the German group of sausages, knockwurst is traditionally made with beef and is sometimes smoked. Bratwurst or your basic beef frankfurter is the best substitute.

K

Food Foibles

If you're going to purée kiwi for a fruit sauce, use either a food processor fitted with a steel blade or push it through a food mill. But do not use a blender; you'll pulverize the seeds, which will make the purée an unappetizing gray color.

kohlrabi (*kol-RAH-bee*)   A root vegetable, kohlrabi, like beets, is a "two-fer." You can quickly stir-fry the leaves like you would beet greens or turnip greens, and you can eat the round globe raw or cooked. The taste is a cross between cabbage and turnip, but sweeter than either. For raw kohlrabi, substitute celeriac, Jerusalem artichoke, or jicama. For cooked, parsnips or Jerusalem artichokes are your best choices, but they'll have to be cooked longer than kohlrabi.

kosher salt   *See* salt.

Kümmel (*KOO-mull*)   *See* liqueur.

kumquat   These tiny fruit look like miniature oval oranges, and they're prized for their edible peel more than their rather dry fruit. Most often they're used as a garnish, in which case substitute slices of navel orange. For marmalades and other cooked dishes, use mandarin oranges.

L

lager   *See* beer.

lamb   Lamb is inherently far more flavorful than beef and has a rosy richness that fills the house with a wonderful aroma as it cooks. Smaller than beef and pork, a full-grown lamb of about 8 months old rarely weighs more than 115 pounds. The meat is so tender that almost all cuts may be roasted, even when the animal is mature.

Spring lamb comes from animals younger than 5 months, and *lamb* is from animals under 1 year. *Mutton* comes from animals from 1 to 2 years old and should only be braised or stewed, as all cuts require tenderizing.

To find the best substitutions, consult the following table, and look for a cut that's recommended for the same cooking method.

Lamb at a Glance

Lamb	Description	Cooking Method(s)
Arm chops	less tender	braise, broil
Baby lamb	15 to 20 lb.	roast at 450°F for 10 to 12 min. per lb.
Blade chops	less tender	braise, broil
Crown roast	rack in a circle	roast
English chops	thick chop with kidney attached	broil, sauté

Lamb	Description	Cooking Method(s)
Kebabs	boned and cubed leg	grill, broil
Leg	with bone or boneless	roast
Leg, butterflied	cut open	grill, broil
Loin chops	meat on either side of a T-shape bone	grill, broil
Noisettes	boned loin chops	roast, grill, broil
Rack	attached rib chops	roast
Shank	lower part of leg	braise
Shoulder	with bone or boneless	braise, roast

Another quandary when cooking lamb or any meat is how much you need per person, especially if you're substituting a cut with bones for one without. The following table helps you determine how much you'll need.

Lamb per Person

Cut	With Bone	Without Bone
Leg	12 oz.	8 oz.
Rack	1 rack per 2 people	n/a
Rib chops	3 double	n/a
Shanks	1 (12 to 16 oz.)	n/a
Shoulder chops	2 (1 in.)	n/a
Shoulder roast	12 oz.	8 oz.

lamb, ground   Ground beef is the best alternative, although you won't get the rich flavor.

lard   Snowy white and sold in 1-pound blocks, lard is rendered pork fat, so it's predominately saturated fat. It produces very flaky and tender baked goods, which is why it's still used in many parts of the world. You can use butter instead, but both stick margarine and vegetable shortening contain a high percentage of trans fat, so avoid those. *See also* fats and oils.

Laroda plum   *See* plum.

lavash (*lah-VASH*)   This Armenian flatbread is used as a wrapper for sandwiches and other foods. A flour tortilla is the best substitute; try to find thin ones. When lavash dries out, it has the texture of a water cracker, which can be used as a fill-in.

lavender   This aromatic herb of the mint family is associated most closely with Provence, and it's almost never alone as a seasoning. It's a component of herbes de Provence, and that mix can always be used.

leaf lettuce   *See* lettuce.

leek   This member of the onion family looks like a scallion on steroids, but its flavor is more delicate. Only the white and palest of green portions of leeks are eaten. A combination of ½ scallions and ½ shallots delivers a similar flavor.

Leicester cheese   *See* cheese.

lemon   In addition to adding its lip-pursing tart flavor to foods, freshly squeezed lemon juice is also used to prevent discoloration and as an acid in salad dressing. While the flavor is different, freshly squeezed lime juice is your best alternative. For salads, a proportion of ½ cider vinegar and ½ water delivers the same acidity. If a recipe calls for "juice of 1 lemon," use 3 tablespoons bottled lemon juice as a sub.

lemon balm   Although *lemon* is in its name, the flavor of this herb is like that of an herbaceous mint.

1 TB. chopped fresh lemon balm = 2 tsp. chopped fresh mint + 1 tsp. chopped fresh oregano

lemon curd   Used in Great Britain as an alternative to jelly or jam on bread and as a filling for tarts, lemon curd is a thick mixture made from lemon juice, eggs, butter, and sugar. It's sold in jars in most supermarkets. Prepared lemon pudding can be used in the same measure.

lemon extract   This is most often used in baking recipes to add both flavor and aroma. Use 2 teaspoons freshly grated lemon zest for 1 teaspoon lemon extract.

lemon pepper   The name is a misnomer; salt is the primary ingredient in this mixed seasoning used most often for poultry and seafood.

1 tsp. lemon pepper = $^1/_2$ tsp. salt + $^1/_4$ tsp. coarsely ground black pepper + pinch grated lemon zest

lemon zest   *See* zest.

lemongrass   Technically an herb, lemongrass has a strong citrus flavor with a spicy finish. It's used in many Asian cuisines, especially Thai and Vietnamese, and it looks like a fibrous scallion. Only the lower bulb is used.

1 stalk lemongrass = 1 TB. freshly squeezed lemon juice + 1 tsp. grated lemon zest + $^1/_4$ tsp. ground ginger

lentil   Any color of lentils can be substituted for any other; their flavor is the same. The only other legume that cooks in the same time and does not require any presoaking are split peas; the yellow (Canadian) ones resemble lentils more than the classic green.

lettuce   We are long past the days when salad meant a wedge of iceberg lettuce; the contents of the salad bowl today can be as colorful as that of the fruit bowl. Here are some of the types of salad lettuces you can pick up in the produce section:

arugula (or *rocket*)   Small, tender, and pungent, the elongated, smooth, dark green leaves have fairly long stems and grow in small clusters. Arugula is excellent when combined with sweet or bitter greens, adding a decidedly spicy taste.

Belgian endive   The spear-shaped leaves form a small, compact head. They're pale green, almost white, with slightly ruffled, pale yellow edges. The texture is crisp and juicy and the flavor pleasantly bitter. A full-bodied dressing, especially a sweet one, balances this green's slightly bitter taste.

bibb   Bibb is a small version of Boston lettuce, although the loosely furled green leaves often are darker and have a crunchier texture. Mild dressing complements its delicate, sweet flavor.

Boston (or *butter*)   Its moderately sized, loosely furled leaves form a tight core. They're pale green (almost white near the center rib), soft, and delicate. It's best to use a light dressing, such as a vinaigrette, on this mild green.

curly endive   A type of chicory, curly endive has large, lacy (almost prickly), dark green outer leaves and tender, pale green inner ones. (Some types of chicory are pale green and known as frisée.) The outer leaves often are blanched and served warm or cold, with olive oil and lemon juice or vinegar. Use the inner leaves in salads. This green is good when paired with other bitter greens and topped with a robust vinaigrette.

escarole   A member of the chicory family, its large head has dark green outer leaves that are loosely packed and slightly furled. It has a tender, pale green inner heart. The outer leaves can be blanched and the inner ones used in salad. The flavor is bitter with a slightly sweet edge. Escarole is excellent in mixed green salads.

frisée   This is the mildest of the chicory family and has pale green, slender curly leaves with the heart almost a yellowish-white. Frisée is used in some traditional French salads. Hearts of curly endive can be used as a substitute.

iceberg   The best-selling salad green in the United States, iceberg lettuce is appreciated primarily for its crunchy texture, making it a nice addition to a salad with arugula, escarole, or chicory. It goes well with full-flavored dressings.

leaf (or *red leaf*)   Leaf lettuce's frilly edged leaves are delicate in texture and flavor, and it's available in green- and red-tipped types. Leaf lettuces are best in a mixed salad with a mild, lightly textured dressing.

mâche (or *corn salad*)   A dark green, delicate cluster of leaves that grows from a small center stem, this green is a true specialty item—expensive and very perishable. Mild and sweet, it works well with a vinaigrette.

mizuna   Mizuna is one of the prettiest of salad greens; its jagged dark green leaves look like those from a dandelion with a delicate texture. However, its flavor boasts a hint of mustardlike pungency.

oakleaf Its large leaves resemble those of an oak, hence the name, and are arranged loosely around a central core. Available in a red leaf (also called ruby) and pale green leaf. A light dressing complements its sweet flavor.

radicchio Developed in Italy, radicchio is a member of the chicory family. The heads range from golf ball to grapefruit size. The beautiful white-veined leaves vary from bright red to dark maroon. The flavor is rather bitter, and it's good when combined with other bitter greens. In Italy, it's served braised, grilled, or wilted, often with a splash of vinegar and oil.

romaine Also called Cos (after the Greek island where it originated), romaine lettuce has crisp, dark green oblong leaves with a thick white rib down the center. The inner leaves usually are pale yellow-green and more tender than the outer ones. Its flavor is a little more than those of other mild greens. Romaine stands up well to bold combinations, such as the cheese, greens, and anchovies typical of classic Caesar salad. It also adds interest to a mixed green salad. The outer leaves often are cooked.

watercress A member of the cabbage family, watercress's sprigs have 5- to 6-inch crisp, succulent stems with tender green leaves. Watercress is quite popular for its peppery flavor, so it's often used as a garnish and as an ingredient in salads with bitter greens.

Making substitutions for some ingredients is difficult if you want to retain the character of the finished dish, but this is hardly a problem with lettuces. Using the following table, pick a lettuce that has the same characteristics as one specified in a recipe.

Lettuces at a Glance

Lettuce	Texture	Flavor
Arugula	tender	pungent
Belgian endive	crisp	slightly bitter
Bibb	very tender	mild

continues

Lettuces at a Glance   (continued)

Lettuce	Texture	Flavor
Boston (butter)	very tender	mild
Curly endive	crisp	bitter
Escarole	crisp	bitter
Frisée	crisp	bitter
Iceberg	crisp	very mild
Leaf (red leaf)	crisp tender	mild
Mâche (corn salad)	tender	mild
Mizuna	tender	slightly pungent
Oakleaf	tender	mild
Radicchio	tender leaves with crisp veins	slightly bitter
Romaine (Cos)	tender leaves with crisp veins	fairly mild
Watercress	tender leaves on crisp stalks	peppery, pungent

light cream   *See* cream.

Lillet (*lee-lay*)   *See* apéritif.

lily buds   *See* mushroom, Asian dried.

lima bean   These pale green, elliptical, flat beans come in small and large (Fordhook) sizes. They have a delicate, sweet flavor and are high in starch. For baby lima beans, green peas, edamame, and cooked garbanzo beans are your best choices. Fava beans (peeled) are the best stand-ins for Fordhooks. *See also* beans, dried.

lime   Lime juice delivers a more distinctive flavor than lemon juice, although it serves the same function of preventing discoloration. Freshly squeezed lemon juice can be substituted in direct proportion. If a recipe calls for "juice of 1 lime," use 1½ to 2 tablespoons bottled lime juice.

lingcod   Despite its name, lingcod is not part of the Atlantic cod family; it's a huge fish from the northern Pacific with dense flesh and a mild flavor. Your best bets: any of the cod species or halibut.

lingonberry   Famed in Scandinavian countries both fresh and as a jam to serve with game meats, lingonberries are a cousin of our domestic cranberry. Cranberries are the best substitute, although add sugar because they're much tarter. Fresh red currants also work.

linguiça (*lin-GWEE-sah*)   This pork sausage flavored with paprika and garlic is Portuguese in origin, so its best substitute is chorizo, from the other half of the Iberian peninsula.

linguine (*lin-GWEE-knee*)   *See* pasta, dried.

liqueur (*leh-kour*)   Liqueurs are distilled spirits that are flavored and sweetened, and that's about where the similarities end. Liqueurs have been around for centuries; Bénédictine, flavored with more than 20 herbs, was first produced in a Norman abbey in 1510. Most liqueurs are based on neutral alcohol, some are based on brandy, and others begin as a spirit. The liqueur market is well established, but it's exploded over the past century and continues to grow at a rapid pace. You can find generic liqueurs, usually labeled *crème de (whatever the flavor)*, and proprietary brands. Here are the major families of liqueurs; any within a group can be substituted for any other:

> *anise*   Made with anise seeds, all these liqueurs have a strong licorice flavor. Greek ouzo has many producers, but the production from many other countries is proprietary. Pernod and Ricard are two popular brands of French pastis, Sambuca and Galliano are Italian, and Herbsaint is American. If you don't want to use a liqueur to deliver the anise flavor, substitute 3 star anise pods per 2 tablespoons anise liqueur while cooking.

> *berry*   Crème de cerise is the generic cherry liqueur, and Cherry Heering, Maraschino liqueur, and Cherry Marnier are the best-known brand names. Crème de cassis, a black currant liqueur, adds a berry note to the French apéritif called a kir, and the best-known among the raspberry liqueurs is Chambord.

> *coffee*   Kahlúa and Tía Maria, both from Mexico, are the leading brands in this category, and Starbucks has also entered the market. For coffee flavor without the jolt, substitute 2 teaspoons instant espresso

powder and 1 tablespoon granulated sugar dissolved in 2 tablespoons boiling water for every 2 tablespoons coffee liqueur.

herbal and vegetal   This family has myriad additions to give them distinctive flavors from the garden, so let's look at each separately:

◆ *Advocaat* is a Dutch liqueur flavored with egg yolks and vanilla.

   1 TB. Advocaat = 1 TB. brandy + dash vanilla extract

◆ Bénédictine is cognac into which more than two dozen herbs and spices are added. Use brandy or brandy extract.

◆ Drambuie is based on Scotch whisky flavored with honey and herbs. Irish Mist is a similar liqueur made with Irish whiskey.

   1 TB. Drambuie = 1 TB. Scotch + 1 tsp. honey

◆ Kümmel is flavored with caraway seeds, cumin, and fennel.

   1 TB. Kümmel = 1 TB. vodka + 1 tsp. crushed caraway seeds

nut   There are only a few leaders in this category; Amaretto adds a sweet almond flavor, Frangelico is made from hazelnuts, and Nocino has a walnut flavor. These liqueurs all add a delicious nut flavor to foods; a substitute for any of them is ¼ teaspoon pure almond extract per 1 tablespoon nut liqueur.

orange   Among the fruits, orange liqueurs are the most popular. Most people think Grand Marnier, a brandy-based liqueur, is the best for sipping or flavoring dishes such as soufflés and custard sauces. For mixing into a drink or fruit salad, consider Cointreau, Curaçao, Mandarin Napoleon, and Triple Sec. Another substitution is ¼ teaspoon orange oil per 1 tablespoon liqueur.

liquor   *See* spirits.

littleneck clam   *See* clam.

liver   Of all the organ meats, liver—especially calf liver and chicken liver—is the most widely accepted. Chicken and calves' livers can be substituted for one another in any recipe; however, chicken livers take longer to cook because they're thicker. If substituting beef liver or pork liver, increase the amount of seasoning in the dish to compensate for the more assertive flavor.

liverwurst   This is a large category of German sausages that always includes some sort of liver. The best substitute is any sort of French pâté that includes liver or chicken livers.

lobster   King (or queen) of the crustaceans, nothing substitutes for a boiled or steamed lobster delivered to the table still in its shell. Most supermarkets carry frozen lobster tails, which weigh about 8 ounces each, about the same weight as the meat from a 1-pound lobster removed from its shell. Shrimp or prawns can be substituted for any sautéed lobster dish. In soups, substitute crab. Monkfish, sometimes called "poor man's lobster," has a similar sweet flavor and texture.

loganberry   This succulent fruit is another berry hybrid, created in California in the late nineteenth century. Yet another hybrid, boysenberries, is closest in flavor, or you can always substitute blackberries, the parent fruit.

London broil   *See* beef.

long-grain rice   *See* rice.

lotus root   Unfortunately, there's no direct substitute for lotus root, prized both raw and cooked in Asian cooking. The flavor of lotus root, which is shaped like a boat bumper and covered with a light tan skin, is mild and the texture is crispy. Jicama and Jerusalem artichokes are the closest vegetables.

lovage   This cousin of celery is actually the source of celery seeds, and its crispy stalks taste like strong celery. The leaves are used as seasoning, and the ribs are cooked.

  1 TB. lovage leaves = 3 TB. celery leaves

  3 lovage ribs, cooked = 5 celery ribs, cooked with ¼ tsp. celery seed

low-fat milk   *See* milk.

lox   *See* salmon, smoked.

lychee (*LEE-chee*)   These sweet, ivory-colored, very juicy fruit are about the size of a walnut, and they're covered with a thin bumpy red shell from which they're popped out. If fresh aren't available, it's better to use canned than dried; or peel sweet green grapes. Dried lychee nuts taste like a cross between dried figs and raisins, both of which can be used in their place.

macadamia nut   These sweet and buttery nuts are synonymous with Hawaii. Brazil nuts, almonds, and cashews are your best substitutions, as they share the same sweet aftertaste.

macaroni   *See* pasta, dried.

macaroon   These delicate meringue cookies are frequently flavored with almonds, so amaretti are your best bet. Mandlebrot would work, too, although they're heavier.

mace   This aromatic spice is ground from the skin that covers nutmeg seeds, so nutmeg is certainly closest in both aroma and flavor. Cinnamon or apple pie spice can be used at the same level, but if you're using allspice, use ½ the amount.

mâche(*mahsh*)   *See* lettuce.

mackerel   A cold-water fish with a high oil content and assertive flavor, mackerel is good both fresh and smoked. Bluefish is the best substitute for fresh; either smoked bluefish or kippered herring are good choices for smoked mackerel.

Madeira (*mah-DEER-ah*)   *See* wine, fortified.

mahi mahi   Mahi mahi was once a treat only enjoyed in Hawaii, but air transport has made it possible for us to enjoy its firm, off-white flesh with a sweet flavor anywhere. Swordfish, halibut, and other "meaty" fish are the best alternatives.

Malbec (*MAHL-beck*)   *See* wine, red.

malt vinegar   *See* vinegar.

manchego (*mahn-CHEE-goh*)   *See* cheese.

Mandarin Napoleon   *See* liqueur.

mandarin orange   What differentiates this category of citrus fruit, which includes the delicate clementine as well as the larger tangerine, is that the peels slip off easily. Navel oranges are your best choice if you can't find mandarins.

Mandarin pancake   Sometimes called Chinese pancakes, these thin crêpes are used to wrap foods like moo shu dishes or Peking duck. Flour tortillas—the thinner the better—can stand in at any time.

mandelbrot (*MAN-dull-brot*)   These crispy, dry cookies usually flavored with almonds are like Italian almond biscotti, which are usually easier to find and taste the same.

mango   Mango is the most popular fruit in the tropics, with its fragrant orange-yellow pulp and luscious creamy texture. For both color and flavor, papaya, peaches, and nectarines are your best options. But do look at the refrigerated case in the produce department; many producers are now packing fresh mangoes in water.

M

manicotti (*man-ih-COT-tee*)   *See* pasta, dried.

maple sugar   Maple sugar delivers even more sweetness than granulated cane sugar because the syrup from which it comes is so sweet.

1 cup maple sugar = ¾ cup firmly packed light brown sugar + ¼ tsp. pure maple extract

maple syrup   Those first colonists were lucky that the Native Americans taught them about tapping the sap of dormant maple trees; sugar was a precious commodity. Honey or light molasses works as an alternative with ½ teaspoon pure maple extract added.

Maraschino   *See* liqueur.

margarine   This fat was developed as an alternative to butter, and until the knowledge of trans fats was known, margarine was considered a healthful alternative. It's not any healthier than butter, so always use unsalted butter in its place. *See also* fats and oils.

marinara sauce (*mah-ree-NAH-rub*)   This herbed tomato sauce usually contains herbs and garlic. Use any pasta or pizza sauce with a tomato base in its place, or make your own in minutes.

marjoram (*MAHR-jor-um*)   This grayish-green herb is a first cousin to oregano, but with a milder flavor that makes it a good choice for meat dishes.

1 TB. chopped fresh marjoram = 2 tsp. chopped fresh oregano or 1 TB. chopped fresh parsley + ¹/₂ tsp. dried oregano

marmalade   Marmalade usually refers to a citrus preserve that contains the rind as well as the fruit. Substitute preserves or jam as long as the flavor is compatible.

marrow   Marrow is the fat tissue found in the center of animals' leg bones that's used to enrich sauces. Butter does the same thing.

marsala (*mahr-SAH-lah*)   *See* wine, fortified.

marzipan (*MAHR-zi-pahn*)   A sweetened almond paste, marzipan is used as a filling for pastries and as an art medium; it can be rolled into shapes and painted with food coloring. Years ago it was difficult to find in supermarkets, so I made it myself.

Yield: 3 cups

5 cups blanched almonds
3 cups granulated sugar

⅔ cup water
¾ tsp. pure almond extract

Grind almonds in a food processor fitted with a steel blade until they're a powder. Set aside. Combine sugar and water in a saucepan, and bring to a boil over medium-high heat. Cook until sugar dissolves, add almonds and almond extract, and cook, stirring constantly, for 5 minutes or until mixture forms a mass. Remove the pan from the heat, and transfer mixture to a sheet pan. Knead with a wooden spoon when hot and then with the palm of your hand until smooth. Store for up to 5 days, wrapped in plastic wrap to prevent drying out.

masa harina (*MAH-sah har-EEN-ah*)　*See* cornmeal.

mascarpone (*mah-skahr-POH-neh*)　A rich and thick fresh Italian cheese, mascarpone is used sweetened the way we'd use cream cheese, but it's richer.

1 lb. mascarpone = ½ lb. cream cheese + ½ lb. unsalted butter (Soften both cream cheese and butter, and beat them together until light and fluffy.)

matzo (*MAHT-zuh*)　Jews eat this flour-and-water unleavened ceremonial bread with the texture of a crisp cracker during Passover, and for that occasion, there is no substitute. If using matzo as a cracker, traditional English water crackers or Armenian lavash (after it's dried out) are similar.

matzo meal　Just as breadcrumbs come from crushing bread, matzo meal comes from crushing matzo. They come in medium consistency for foods like matzo balls and a finer texture used to make cakes for Passover.

1 cup matzo meal – 3 or 4 slices matzo, crushed in a food processor fitted with a steel blade; 1 cup cracker crumbs; or 1 cup plain breadcrumbs

Maui onion　*See* onion.

mayonnaise　If you find that the ever-present bottle is empty, don't fret. It's easy to make yourself.

M

Yield: 1½ cups

2 large egg yolks, at room temperature	2 TB. white wine vinegar
Salt and freshly ground white pepper	1 tsp. Dijon mustard
	1¼ cups vegetable oil

Combine egg yolks, salt, pepper, vinegar, and Dijon mustard in a blender. Blend on high speed for 30 seconds or until thick and lemon-colored. Scrape down the sides of the blender jar, and blend for 15 seconds more. Remove the stopper from the jar, and at high speed, drizzle ½ of vegetable oil through the hole. Then add remaining oil in a thin stream. Adjust seasoning, and scrape mixture into a container. Refrigerate until ready to use.

Maytag blue *See* cheese.

Melba toast These crisp rounds are thin slices of thoroughly toasted French bread. Italian crostini or bruschetta are similar, as are bagel chips; they're made from bagels instead of French bread.

melon Thirst-quenching because they're more than 90 percent water, ripe melons are wonderful eaten by themselves, in fruit salads, as sorbets, or with other foods. Now available all year round, melons are most plentiful in the summer. Most melon, except watermelon, can be substituted for one another, but be sure the color is compatible with the planned use.

cantaloupe It's important to select ripe cantaloupes; they have no stored starches to convert to sugar, so they'll get softer but not sweeter. The flesh is a soft orange and should be firm and very fragrant. The flavor of a ripe cantaloupe is sweet; over-ripe cantaloupe are mealy. The stem end should smell sweet and give a little when pressed, and the netting should be clear.

casaba These large winter melons have coarse, ridged, dark-green to deep-yellow rinds, and a globe shape with a slightly pointed stem end. The flesh is creamy white or pale green, sweet but mild, and juicy. The stem end should smell sweet and give a little when pressed.

crenshaw A winter melon, the rind of this oval-shape melon is dark green and turns light yellow as it ripens. The flesh is a bright coral color, with a sweet flavor and a spicy aroma.

honeydew Probably the most popular of the winter melons, the honeydew is large, with a pale green rind that turns light yellow as it ripens. The flesh of the honeydew is light green to white and has a mild, sweet flavor.

Persian Like the cantaloupe, the Persian melon has distinct netting. Large and nearly round, it has a smooth, gray-green rind under the light gray netting. The flesh is a deep salmon color, with a full, sweet flavor.

Santa Claus Another winter melon, the Santa Claus is smaller than the casaba, with a mottled dark-green and yellow rind that turns greener as it ripens. The flesh is pale green and tastes somewhat like honeydew.

watermelon A classic summer staple, the watermelon is distinctive for its large size and bright red flesh. The rind is green and can be flecked with yellow.

Food Foibles

It's important to wash all melons with soap and water before cutting them to avoid transferring illness-causing bacteria on the rind to the flesh when you cut into the melon.

Merlot (*mehr-low*)   See wine, red.

mesclun (*MEHS-clun*)   Sometimes called salad mix or baby green mix, this mélange of colorful greens always includes different shapes and colors. Radicchio, mizuna, mâche, arugula, and bits of leaf lettuce are frequently included, so you can mix your own.

Metaxa (*meh-TAHX-ah*)   See brandy.

Mexican chocolate   Mexicans invented hot chocolate, and their version of the sweetened base is flavored with cinnamon and ground almonds.

$1/4$ lb. Mexican chocolate, melted = $1/4$ lb. bittersweet chocolate, melted + $1/2$ cup ground almonds + $1/4$ tsp. ground cinnamon + $1/8$ tsp. pure almond extract

Meyer lemon   Chefs who were part of the "California cuisine" movement in the 1980s popularized this sweeter form of lemon that originated in China. The lemons are larger and rounder than true lemons, and the yellow-orange skin is edible.

1 cup Meyer lemon juice = $1/2$ cup freshly squeezed lemon juice + $1/4$ cup freshly squeezed grapefruit juice + $1/4$ cup freshly squeezed orange juice

milk   Milk from dairy cows is the overwhelming majority of what we drink, but goat's milk and sheep's milk are both rich in fat and protein and can be substituted in equal volume. Cow's milk is around 87 percent water, $3 1/2$ percent protein (primarily caseine), and 5 percent carbohydrates or lactose, the milk sugar. The good news is that when the fat is cut back in

M

milk, all the nutrients remain the same. To go the other way and create whole milk from skim milk, add 2 tablespoons heavy cream to each ⅞ cup skim milk.

Milk at a Glance*

Milk	Calories	Fat Content
Evaporated, skim	198	4 g
Evaporated, whole	338	20 g
Low-fat, 1 percent	108	4 g
Low-fat, 2 percent	121	5 g
Skim	86	3 g
Whole	150	8 g

Values per 8-oz. serving.

milk, sweetened condensed   Used for baking and other desserts, this product sold in 14-ounce cans was introduced in the mid-nineteenth century. It's widely available, but it's easy to replicate the taste and thick texture.

Yield: 1¾ cups

1⅓ cups instant nonfat, dry
  milk
1¼ cups granulated sugar

½ cup boiling water
3 TB. melted butter

Combine dry milk, sugar, boiling water, and melted butter in a blender, and process until smooth. Store refrigerated for up to 1 week.

millet   This healthful grain has a rather bland flavor, and it's most often boiled like rice. Quinoa, bulgur, and buckwheat groats can be substituted.

mint   Mint is one of the most versatile herbs; it's equally at home as a jelly with roast leg of lamb, in a Middle Eastern tabbouleh salad, or part of a chocolate sauce. There are more than 30 varieties of mint, and they can be used interchangeably because they all deliver a strong but sweet menthol aftertaste. For sweet dishes, substitute 1 tablespoon crème de menthe for each 2 teaspoons fresh mint. For savory dishes, add ⅛ teaspoon mint extract for each 1 tablespoon fresh mint.

mirin (*meer-in*)   This sweet Japanese rice wine is used extensively in cooking.

> *¼ cup mirin = ¼ cup red vermouth, sweet marsala, plum wine, or sweet sherry, or ¼ cup sake + 1 TB. honey*

mirliton (*MEER-leh-tohn*)   *See* chayote.

miso (*mee-soh*)   Miso is a fermented bean paste that's a staple of Japanese cooking; it's almost the equivalent of bullion powder. Chinese black bean or sweet bean paste are the best alternatives.

mizuna (*mee-zoo-nah*)   *See* lettuce.

molasses   Molasses is the liquid that's left over from refining sugar cane, and its flavor is in light and dark brown sugar.

> *1 cup molasses = 1 cup dark corn syrup, 1 cup honey, or 1 cup dark brown sugar + ⅓ cup water, heated to dissolve sugar*

monkfish   It's hard to find a substitute for the almost sweet flavor of monkfish, or "poor man's lobster." Grouper and halibut have similar textures if you don't want to spring for the cost of lobster.

Monterey Jack cheese   *See* cheese.

Montrachet cheese (*mohn-rah-shay*)   *See* cheese.

morel (*more-ell*)   *See* mushroom, wild.

mortadella (*mor-tah-DELL-ah*)   This Italian cold cut is basically bologna flecked with cubes of fat and sometimes pistachio nuts. Bologna is your obvious substitute.

Moscato (*moos-KAH-toh*)   *See* wine, dessert.

mostaccioli (*moh-stah-chee-OH-lay*)   *See* pasta, dried.

mozzarella (*moh-t'zeh-REL-ah*)   *See* cheese.

Muenster cheese (*MUHN-star*)   *See* cheese.

muesli (*MEOW-slee*)   Raw and toasted grains along with nuts and dried fruits are included in this healthful breakfast cereal invented in the nineteenth century. Granola has most of the same ingredients.

Toque Tips

For an easy and delicious fruit dessert topping, mix either muesli or granola with a bit of melted butter.

mulato   *See* chilies, dried.

mulberry   Don't look for mulberries in the market because you won't find them; these sweet-tart berries are not cultivated in this country, but they do grow wild from New England to Florida. Blackberries are your best bet for replicating the look and taste.

mullet   This fish with a relatively high oil content and firm flesh runs in the same warm waters along the Gulf Coast as red snapper. Grouper and sea bass deliver the closest delicate flavor.

Muscadet (*muss-kah-day*)   *See* wine, white.

Muscat (*muss-kaht*)   *See* wine, dessert.

mushroom, dried Asian   In addition to dried shiitake mushrooms, which are now available almost everywhere, certain dried mushrooms are used in Asian dishes, such as tree ear (sometimes called tree fungus or wood ear) and lily buds (also called tiger lily buds). They can be used interchangeably, and dried shiitake mushrooms can be substituted at any time. Dried shiitakes won't grow in size, but tree ear and lily buds expand greatly when hydrated.

mushroom, white White mushrooms are as much a produce staple today as carrots and celery, but if your market runs out, crimini (sometimes dubbed "baby portobello") are the best alternative. If your only alternative is canned mushrooms, don't. They have an unappetizing flavor and texture.

Toque Tips

To slice mushrooms quickly and easily and ensure even slices, use an egg slicer. Don't use a food processor fitted with a slicing disc; the mushrooms won't create pretty slices.

mushroom, wild Exactly what constitutes a "wild mushroom" is getting more and more difficult to define because many varieties of wild mushrooms are being cultivated. Wild mushrooms add an earthy richness to dishes, and it's easy to substitute them in recipes calling for white mushrooms for soups, stews, or sautéed as a vegetable garnish. In general, 1 pound fresh wild mushrooms delivers the same flavor as 3 ounces dried wild mushrooms. For varieties that have both, use that as a rule of thumb and then use fresh mushrooms for volume.

Here are the ones you'll commonly find:

chanterelle (or *girolle*) Called "trumpets" due to their shape, most chanterelle are an exotic golden color, although the colors range from a creamy white to a warm red/gold. The flavor is nutty and meaty, and they come in just about every size from the size of your thumb to up to 12 inches wide and weighing 2 pounds. Chanterelles freeze well but lose flavor when dried.

crimini These are now easy to find most everywhere, and they're frequently marketed as "baby portobellos." They have a dense, earthy flavor not as strong as that of most wild mushrooms and can be used interchangeably with white mushrooms in almost all dishes. Either white mushrooms or fresh portobellos are the best options.

enoki These light and crisp mushrooms with a peppery aftertaste are almost always eaten raw as a garnish to salads. They resemble beans sprouts more than other wild mushrooms and have a long, thin, delicate, creamy-colored stem with a puffy little cap. Oyster mushrooms, white mushrooms, or mung bean sprouts are your best choices for substitutions.

morel   These spring mushrooms, which still almost defy cultivation, are about 1 inch long with a tall, hollow, pitted "hat." The colors range from gray to brown to black, depending on where they're grown. Their flavor is rich, nutty, and meaty when cooked, and they should never be eaten raw. Fresh shiitake, chanterelles, or dried morels are alternatives.

oyster   Sometimes referred to as "shellfish of the woods," oyster mushrooms are delicate and translucent mushrooms with a silky consistency. The cap is shaped like a scallop, and they have a graceful appearance, similar to that of a calla lily. Despite the slight aroma of anise, oyster mushrooms have a mild shellfish flavor. Enoki or chanterelles are your best substitutes.

porcini (or *cèpes*)   This mushroom is popular the world over but is very important in Italian cuisine and is used as much dried as fresh. Porcini do not have gills under the cap, but rather a mass of minuscule tubes. Their flavor is earthy and rich and reminiscent of hazelnuts, while the texture remains delicate. The colors range from rusty brown to terra cotta.

portobello   These earthy mushrooms are crimini that have been allowed to grow large, and their meaty texture makes them an excellent substitution for meat when grilling for a vegetarian. Crimini are the best alternative for sautéing, and eggplant is a good choice if grilling.

shiitake   The second most widely cultivated mushroom in the world, shiitake mushrooms have been a popular part of Asian cuisines for centuries. They have a distinctive woodsy-smoky flavor and are moist and fleshy when fresh. They are medium-size to large, umbrella-shaped, floppy tan to dark brown, with a cap that tends to roll inward on the edge. A combination of dried shiitake and fresh crimini mushrooms are your best alternative.

truffles   Round, irregular in shape, with a rough texture, most truffles are as small as a walnut. The black truffle of France is jet black on the interior. The white truffle of Italy is quite famous for its sharp, distinctive, peppery flavor. The earthy, distinctive aroma of truffles is directly related to their flavor. Truffles are best shaved or grated raw onto foods, particularly soups and sauces. Canned truffles are not as wonderful as fresh, but they still add a very indulgent touch to food, and the flavor and aroma are also conveyed with truffle oil. Truffles are not available dried, but both dried morels and porcini add an earthy flavor to foods.

mussels   Some cuisines enjoy mussels raw, but we always eat mussels steamed and sauced simply or elaborately. Soft-shell "steamer" clams and littleneck clams can be prepared in the same ways and take the same amount of time.

Food Foibles

The most important consideration about mussels, like all mollusks, is that they're alive when you cook them. The shells should be tightly closed or close tightly when they're handled. Second is their weight; heavy mussels are probably filled with mud and sand, so go for the lighter ones.

M

mustard   Mustard has long been used as a sharp, pungent seasoning for foods; it adds zest and enhances flavors. The robust flavor of mustard comes out only when the seeds are ground and the powder is mixed with a liquid such as water, vinegar, cider, white wine, or ale. Here are the various ways it comes:

dry   The technique for producing dry mustard has changed little since the eighteenth century: seeds are ground to produce a powder. Frequently wheat flour is added to the seeds, as well as turmeric for color, and some sugar, salt, and spices. Dry mustard also acts as a preservative and is often included in pickle and chutney recipes. To bring out its flavor, dry mustard must be mixed with a liquid.

   1 tsp. dry mustard = 2 tsp. prepared mustard

flavored   Flavored mustards, enhanced by the addition of an herb, spice, or other flavoring, have proliferated during the past decade. They can be gently imbued with honey or with delicate herbs such as basil, tarragon, chives, or mint; with spicier ingredients such as green peppercorns, chilies, cumin, or ginger; or with fruits such as lemon, lime, or berries.

> *1 cup flavored mustard = 1 cup prepared mustard + 3 TB. herbs and spices or 2 TB. chilies or grated ginger*

prepared   The use of white (mild) or brown (stronger) seed determines the character of a mustard. For mild mustard, the seed coat, or hull, is completely or partially left on; for strong mustard, it's sifted out. Mild prepared mustards contain a higher percentage of the hull and no less than 20 percent dry mustard powder. Bordeaux, Beaujolais, and whole-grain mustards are the most commonly available mild types.

American mustards are made from the milder, ground white mustard seeds, blended with vinegar, sugar, spices, and often turmeric, which is the source of the characteristic yellow color.

The most popular strong mustard is Dijon. Made from brown mustard seeds, it's mixed with white wine and unfermented grape juice.

> *1 TB. prepared mustard = 1 tsp. dry mustard + 2 tsp. white wine or vinegar*

whole-grain   Whole-grain mustards are mild Dijon mustards made of partially crushed and ground brown seeds, blended with vinegar and spices. The most well-known type is moutarde de Meaux, identified by its attractive stoneware jar with a red wax seal. Whole-grain mustard is relatively mild in taste because the hull is not totally removed.

> *¼ cup whole-grain mustard = 3 TB. mustard seed, crushed + 2 TB. white wine or vinegar + salt and freshly ground black pepper*

mustard green   *See* greens.

Toque Tips

The taste of mustard dissipates rapidly from heat, so add mustard at the end of cooking a dish.

mustard seed   Mustard seeds are used in pickling, as well as in mixed spices used to boil fish and seafood.

1 TB. mustard seed = 2 tsp. dry mustard or 1 TB. prepared mustard

mutton   *See* lamb.

naan (*nahn*)   This lightly leavened bread is a staple of Indian cooking. It's traditionally baked in a high-heat tandoor oven, which gives it a slightly smoky flavor. Either pita bread or flour tortillas can be substituted, as can other Indian breads or Armenian lavash.

nam pla   *See* fish sauce.

Napa cabbage   Although this cabbage is named for California's Napa Valley, it's used primarily in Asian cooking. Bok choy is the best stand-in; it shares the same sweet flavor and crisp texture. Swiss chard or Savoy cabbage are other possibilities, but they have a stronger flavor.

nasturtium (*nas-TUR-chum*)   This plant is prized for its colorful, edible flowers as well as its delicate leaves, which have a slightly peppery flavor. Species of edible pansies and marigolds can be used to add color to your salads, and either arugula or watercress can be substituted for the leaves.

navel orange   *See* orange.

navy bean   *See* beans, dried.

Nebbiolo (*neh-bee-YOH-low*)   *See* wine, red.

nectarine   The nectarine is closely related to the peach but with a richer flavor and a nonfuzzy skin. They come in both clingstone and freestone varieties. Peaches, although they need peeling, are the best substitute, with fresh apricots a distant second place.

Food Foibles

While peaches can be used in place of nectarines, the reverse is not always the case. Nectarines have a tendency to fall apart when cooked, so keep that in mind before you use them.

Neufchâtel (*newf-sha-tell*)   This fresh cheese from France has the flavor and texture of cream cheese, but with less fat. Cream cheese is your best substitution.

New Mexico green   *See* chilies, fresh.

New Mexico red   *See* chilies, fresh.

New York steak   *See* beef.

Nocino (*noh-SEE-noh*)   *See* liqueur.

nonfat milk   *See* milk.

nonpareil   These colored sugar dots are used to decorate cakes and cookies. Use miniature chocolate-covered candies, colored sugars, or sprinkles in their place.

noodles   *See* egg noodles.

nopale (*noh-PAH-lay*)   These leaves from the prickly pear cactus have long been part of Mexican cooking, and they're now quite easy to find in American supermarkets. Either peel them to remove the thorns as well as the skin or use a green mesh scrubber to sand off the thorns. Then you can sautée or steam the pale green flesh. The flavor is most reminiscent of green beans, and you can substitute chayote squash.

nori (*noh-ree*)   Nori is the green seaweed wrapping used for sushi rolls. Its flavor is only mildly reminiscent of the sea and certainly not fishy! Nori becomes pliable when damp, which is why it rolls so well. Blanched leaves of collard greens or leek leaves are your best alternatives for nori's dark green color, although nothing replicates the flavor.

nougat (*new-gut*)   This sweet and chewy confection popular in Italy and southern France is like a cross between caramel and salt water taffy. It usually contains toasted nuts and occasionally candied fruit, too. Either caramel or taffy are your best alternatives.

nutmeg   The nutmeg is the seed of the fruit, and mace is ground from the coating covering the skin. Nutmeg is always far better if freshly grated; the aroma dissipates quickly. Use either mace or apple pie spice in its place.

Toque Tips

Add nutmeg and mace at the end of the cooking process, because heat diminishes the flavor. And always use freshly grated nutmeg when possible. It has far more aroma and flavor.

N

O

oakleaf lettuce *See* lettuce.

oat This grain is defined by how finely it's milled, and both old-fashioned and quick oats are used to cook basic oatmeal. Irish and Scotch steel-cut oats are larger than old-fashioned oats and take longer to cook. In baking, a crushed breakfast cereal like cornflakes can be substituted in equal volume to oats as a textural addition for cookies. One cup all-purpose flour takes the place of 1⅓ cups oats in batters such as quick breads.

Food Foibles

Both old-fashioned and quick oats can be used in cooking, but don't substitute instant oats. They're *instant* because they're precooked, so in a baked good, they turn into almost a glue.

oat bran This outer casing of oat is very high in fiber and is touted to lower bad cholesterol. Wheat and rice also have bran, or you can substitute wheat germ.

ocean whitefish *See* tilapia.

octopus Octopus is used most frequently in Japanese cooking because a great percentage of the world's harvest is in that country's waters. Squid and cuttlefish can be used in its place and cook in the same amount of time.

offal *See* brains; kidneys; liver; sweetbreads; tongue.

oil *See* fats and oils.

oil, infused   In contemporary cooking, vegetable oils are often infused with flavoring ingredients. In sautéing, the flavor of the ingredients is transferred to the food being cooked; the oil also brings this flavor to salad dressings. To infuse an oil, chop the flavoring ingredient finely, combine with the oil, and allow it to stand for a minimum of 48 hours. If using the oil for sautéing, strain out the particles; leave them in for dressings. *See also* fats and oils.

Making Your Own Infused Oils

Flavor	Add per 2 Cups Vegetable Oil
Chili	3 TB. crushed red pepper flakes
Garlic	3 TB. minced
Ginger	¼ cup grated
Lemon	3 TB. grated zest
Orange	3 TB. grated zest
Oregano	¾ cup, chopped
Rosemary	¾ cup, chopped
Sage	¾ cup, chopped
Thyme	½ cup, chopped

oil, nut   These are the very expensive oils pressed from various aromatic and flavorful nuts, including hazelnuts and walnuts. Any nut oil can be substituted for each other, but don't use Asian sesame oil because the flavor is far stronger. *See also* fats and oils.

okra   Part and parcel of Southern cooking, especially for gumbo, okra was introduced to this continent by African slaves, and the vegetable is used in many ways today. As a green vegetable, substitute green beans or sugar snaps. For fried okra, use fried green tomatoes or nuggets of fried asparagus. Okra also contains a sticky juice that becomes a thickening agent when it's cooked.

2 cups sliced okra = 1 TB. filé powder or 1 TB. cornstarch mixed with 2 TB. cold water

Old Bay seasoning   The bay in question is the Chesapeake, and this seasoning mix was developed to flavor the region's famed blue crabs. Commercial Cajun seasoning has many of the same ingredients.

olive   Cultivated since ancient times, olives are the most popular fruit in the world. Raw olives must be cured in oil, brine, or salt before they can be eaten, and the curing affects their flavor and texture, as does the olives' degree of ripeness when they're picked. Green olives are harvested at early stages of maturity in October; pink olives are really a rosy brown color and are harvested next, to be followed by black olives in December. If garnishing a martini, use cocktail onions; when cooking, try capers for the same salty flavor. If you want olives for eating, the following table provides a guide to olives and their best stand-ins.

Olives at a Glance

Olive	Origin	Substitution
Amphissa (*am-FISS-ah*)	Greece	Kalamata, Gaeta
Arbequina (*ahr-bee-KEEN-ah*)	Spain	Manzanilla
Cerignola (*sir-en-YOH-lah*)	Italy	Manzanilla
Gaeta (*guy-EH-tah*)	Italy	Kalamata
Kalamata (*kal-ah-MAH-tah*)	Greece	Amphissa, Gaeta
Manzanilla (*mahn-zahn-KNEE-yah*)	Spain	Arbequina, Cerignola
Niçoise (*knee-swahz*)	France	Kalamata, Gaeta
Nyon (*knee-yon*)	France	Kalamata, Niçoise
Picholine (*peach-oh-lean*)	France	Manzanilla, Cerignola

olive oil   Olive oil has become a staple in all American kitchens. Its inherent fruity flavor is important to today's popular Mediterranean cuisines, and its high percentage of monounsaturated fat makes it more healthful to use than other oils. Olive oil is made from ripe, crushed olives. Two types of olive oils are available commercially:

extra virgin   This is the first pressing of the olives, which have been cold pressed (no heat added) with no chemicals added to the mixture. In most countries, olive oil must have less than 1 percent acidity to be called *extra virgin*.

pure   This is a blend of virgin and refined olive oil, which is oil that's been extracted from the olives by means other than mechanical or physical. Bruised or too-ripe olives are mixed with chemicals such as caustic soda and heated to 180°F so they don't produce unappealing flavors when pressed into oil.

For general cooking, any flavorless vegetable oil such as corn, canola, or safflower can be substituted. When using an extra-virgin olive oil as a condiment, the best substitution is a nut oil such as walnut or hazelnut. *See also* fats and oils.

Food Foibles

Don't use an expensive extra-virgin olive oil for cooking. The olive particles in the oil will burn and give food an off flavor, and the oil breaks down with high heat.

onion   Perhaps not surprising, onions are bulbs related to leeks and garlic. Usually, the milder the climate in which an onion is grown, the sweeter the onion's flavor. After harvesting, most onion bulbs are left to dry, and the papery outer skin forms. Here are the different onion varieties you'll find:

Bermuda   These large, globelike onions have a very mild flavor, brown skin, and crisp flesh. They're perfect served on sandwiches or on a burger.

common   When a recipe calls for an onion, common onions are usually what you should use. They are fully mature and have either white, yellow, or brown skins and a strong, assertive flavor.

Maui   These Hawaiian onions have very light golden skins. They're so mild they're almost sweet.

pearl   These tiny (½ inch diameter), very round onions are most often boiled, creamed, or served in stews. They are sold with light brown, white, and red skins.

red   These beautiful red-violet onions add a lovely contrasting color to salads and sandwiches, and they can be used for soups and relishes. The color will bleed into dishes when they're cooked, so consider that before substituting them for yellow onions. The flavor isn't constant and can range from sweet to sharp.

Spanish   This is almost a generic term for a large sweet onion with unknown provenance.

Vidalia   This increasingly popular sweet onion grown in Georgia, Texas, and South Carolina is round and has golden brown skin and clear white flesh. Vidalias are extremely sweet and hold their shape well when baked or braised.

Walla Walla   This original sweet onion grown in Washington State has a flavor very similar to the Vidalia.

Any of the sweet onion varieties from Bermuda to Walla Walla can be used interchangeably in a recipe, as can any color of common onion. If substituting a common onion, calculate the amount needed by weight rather than number, as most sweet onions are much larger. Add a few teaspoons sugar to a recipe if using common onions; they're not as sweet.

If making a stew or relish, you can use frozen pearl onions in place of fresh—plus, you'll save the time-consuming step of peeling them. *See also* leek; scallion; shallot.

ono   *See* wahoo.

opakapaka (*oh-pak-ah-PAK-ah*)   This sweet fish from the Hawaiian islands is very difficult to find elsewhere. Both halibut and grouper are excellent alternatives.

opal basil   *See* basil.

orange   Oranges are basically broken into two camps—juicers and eaters. Any of the juicers—Hamlin, Parson Brown, Pineapple, and Valencia—can be used in place of each other. Eating oranges have the ubiquitous navel leading the pack because it's most often seedless. Other eating oranges are the Temple and tangerine, the latter of which is a member of the mandarin orange family. Seville oranges are very bitter and used only for marmalade or as a marinade for fish dishes. If all else fails, substitute a ruby red grapefruit for oranges in fruit salads, although you might need to add a bit more sugar to compensate for the grapefruit's tartness.

orange liqueur   *See* liqueur, orange.

orange roughy   This mildly flavored, firm-fleshed fish is native to the Southern Hemisphere. Flounder, sole, and tilapia are its best Northern Hemisphere equivalents.

orecchiette (*oh-reh-K'YEH-teh*)   *See* pasta, dried.

oregano   We associate oregano with Italian dishes, but it's also used in Greek, French, and Mexican cuisines. Milder marjoram is its first cousin. Substitute 1½ times fresh marjoram for oregano, and if using dried oregano for fresh, use 1 tablespoon fresh for each ¾ teaspoon dried.

orgeat syrup   You'll find this sweet syrup used for tropical rum drinks shelved with the bar mixers in most supermarkets. It has an almond taste and usually has a bit of rose water as an additional flavoring.

½ cup orgeat syrup = ⅔ cup granulated sugar cooked with 3 TB. water until sugar dissolves + ¼ tsp. pure almond extract

orzo (*OAR-zoh*)   *See* pasta, dried.

osetra (*oh-SET-rah*)   *See* caviar.

osso buco (*OH-soh BOO-koh*)   *See* veal.

ostrich   Although it's a bird, ostrich has the meatiness of beef but is more tender. Substitute either beef or dark meat turkey for ostrich. Duck and goose will taste too gamey.

ouzo (*OOU-zoh*)   *See* liqueur.

oxtail   Oxtail comes from a cow or veal calf, and it's very tough, so it needs to be braised for a long time. Short ribs of beef cut into small segments are your best alternative.

oyster   Oysters are named for their place of origin. The best known of the Atlantic oysters is Blue Point; however, Chincoteague and Kent Island in the Chesapeake Bay and Wellfleet on Cape Cod are also well known. Olympia is the most famous West Coast oyster, and the French are known for the Belon.

For oysters on the half-shell, any species can be substituted for one another, or you can substitute hard-shell clams such as littlenecks or cherrystones. Oysters for soups and stews are now available preshucked in many fish departments, which saves considerable time.

12 oysters = 4 oz. meat + ²/₃ cup liquid

1 pt. preshucked oysters = 2 doz.

oyster mushroom   *See* mushroom, wild.

oyster plant   *See* salsify.

oyster sauce   Oyster sauce is a traditional Chinese condiment and cooking sauce, and although it contains oysters, it's not "fishy" in flavor. The oysters and their liquor are cooked with soy sauce and some subtle seasonings until thick, which gives dishes a richness. It's now available in the Asian section of almost all supermarkets, but if you can't find it or you want to make a dish vegetarian, substitute a combination of 50 percent soy sauce and 50 percent black bean sauce.

palm heart   *See* hearts of palm.

palm oil   *See* fats and oils.

pancetta (*pan-CHET-ah*)   *See* bacon.

paneer (*pah-NEER*)   This fresh Indian cheese is similar in flavor to cottage cheese or farmer's cheese, which makes them the best substitutes.

You will have to press the curds to remove excess moisture so the resulting cheese is firm enough to sauté. You can also use firm tofu, but it lacks the cheese flavor.

panettone (*PAH-neh-TOH-neh*)   This Italian yeast bread, rich with butter, eggs, and candied fruit, is traditionally served at Christmas. Brioche and challah can be used in its place, but include some dried fruit in the recipe as well.

panko (*pan-koh*)   These Japanese breadcrumbs are lighter, longer, and less dense than typical breadcrumbs. Their texture creates a deliciously crunchy crust on baked or fried foods. Crushed cornflakes or tortilla chips create a similar coating, as does finely crushed, dried stuffing mix.

papaya   This treat from the tropics has the sweet taste of a melon with nuances of peach. Mango is your best substitute, but you can also use peaches.

Toque Tips

Always save the skin after peeling a papaya and use it in marinades. It contains papain, an enzyme that's used commercially as a tenderizing agent.

pappadam (*PAH-pah-dumm*)   These crispy Indian flatbreads are frequently flavored with spices and herbs. Try bagel chips or pita crisps as a flavored alternative; any crisp cracker works, too.

pappardelle (*pah-pahr-DEH-lay*)   *See* pasta, fresh.

paprika   This kitchen staple used for its vibrant red color more than flavor is made from grinding dehydrated red bell peppers. Most of what is sold in the States is sweet paprika; Hungarian and Spanish paprika both have a little bite.

1 tsp. paprika = ½ tsp. ground red chili

Parmesan cheese   *See* cheese.

parsley   Curley and Italian flat-leaf parsley can be substituted for each other at any time. Chervil is the best alternative if neither parsley is available.

parsnip   The pale tan parsnip is first cousin to the carrot in the family of root vegetables, and they have an even sweeter flavor. If color isn't an issue, use carrots in their place. If you want a pale look for a dish or purée, use celeriac or Jerusalem artichoke.

partridge   *See* game bird.

pasilla chili (*pah-SEE-yah*)   *See* chilies, fresh.

passion fruit   The pulp of this tropical fruit about the size of an egg is a purplish color and contains edible black seeds. It's used most often for sauces or sorbets because the flesh is too soft and liquid to become part of a fruit salad or tart. It's not easy to find a substitution, but puréed blackberries are the closest in color, while mango with a bit of fresh lime juice replicates the flavor.

pasta, dried   Supple, fresh pastas might not be the best match for many hearty sauces, and there's always a place in the pantry for boxes of dried. Good-quality dried pasta is made with a high percentage of high-gluten semolina, the inner part of the grain of hard durum wheat. The gluten gives the pasta resilience and enables it to cook while remaining somewhat firm, the elusive *al dente*.

Many pasta recipes are written for a specific pasta shape; however, you have wide latitude for substitution. What's important is to find a pasta of about the same dimensions that cooks in the same amount of time. The following table lists the types of dried pasta found most often.

Dried Pasta at a Glance

Pasta (Meaning in Italian)	Description	Cooking Time
Anelli (rings)	medium, ridged tubes cut into thin rings	6 to 8 min.
Cannelloni (large pipes)	large cylinders	8 to 10 min. with further baking
Capellini (hair)	thinnest strands	2 to 4 min.
Cavatappi (corkscrews)	short, ridged pasta twisted into a spiral	8 to 10 min.

Pasta (Meaning in Italian)	Description	Cooking Time
Conchiglie (shells)	shells about 1 inch long	8 to 10 min.
Ditalini (little thimbles)	very short, round pieces	6 to 9 min.
Farfalle (butterflies)	flat rectangles pinched in the center to form a bow	10 to 12 min.
Fettuccine (little ribbons)	long, flat ribbon shapes about ¼ inch wide	6 to 9 min.
Fusilli (twisted spaghetti)	long, spring-shape strands	10 to 12 min.
Gemilli (twins)	medium strands woven together and cut into 2-inch lengths	8 to 10 min.
Linguine (little tongues)	thin, slightly flattened solid strands about ⅛ inch wide	6 to 9 min.
Maccheroni (macaroni)	thin, tubular pasta in various widths	8 to 10 min.
Manicotti (small muffs)	thick, ridged tubes	10 to 12 min.
Mostaccioli (small mustaches)	medium-size tubes with angle-cut ends	8 to 10 min.
Orecchiette (ears)	smooth, curved rounds about ½ inch in diameter	6 to 9 min.
Orzo (barley)	tiny, rice-shape	6 to 9 min.
Penne (quills)	small tubes with angle-cut ends	8 to 10 min.
Radiatore (radiators)	short, thick, and ruffled	8 to 10 min.

P

continues

Dried Pasta at a Glance   (continued)

Pasta (Meaning in Italian)	Description	Cooking Time
Rigatoni (large grooved)	thick, ridged tubes about 1½ inches long	10 to 12 min.
Riso (rice)	tiny grains	4 to 6 min.
Rotelle (wheels)	spiral-shape with spokes	8 to 10 min.
Rotini (spirals)	two thick strands twisted	8 to 10 min.
Spaghetti (length of cord)	thin, long strands	8 to 10 min.
Vermicelli (little worms)	thinner than spaghetti	6 to 8 min.
Ziti (bridegroom)	medium-size tubes about 2 inches long	10 to 12 min.

Toque Tips

Use the cooking times given in the preceding table as guidance. The best way to cook pasta is according to the times listed on the individual box; each manufacturer has a slightly different formula and tests its pasta for timing.

pasta, fresh   Maybe you've noticed fresh pasta in your supermarket's refrigerator case. Most of the fresh pastas are strands, ranging in size from angel hair to fettuccine, and any of these can be substituted for each other. You can always use a dried pasta from the preceding table and cook it according to package directions. One exception is pappardelle, which is like a wider strand of fettuccine. For this shape, you can substitute fettuccine or wide egg noodles.

pasta, stuffed   While we tend to think only of ravioli in the category of stuffed pastas, more shapes are made. More important than the shape of the pasta is what's used to stuff it. The stuffing can range from pumpkin to cheese to lobster to prosciutto. Most stuffed pastas are sold refrigerated or frozen, but some manufacturers also sell them dried. Angnoletti and mezzalune are both semi circular in shape. Tortellini and tortelloni can vary in shape; sometimes they're small rectangles and at other times they resemble tiny wontons. Any stuffed pasta can be substituted for another; tortellini are smaller and are usually served in broth, but they can also be sauced.

pastis (*pas-tees*) *See* liqueur, anise.

pastrami The meat used for this cold cut is beef brisket that's rubbed with garlic and spices and then dry-cured and cooked. Corned beef is almost identical in process, although it lacks the spice coating.

pastry cream This thick filling is used in tarts and cream puffs or between layers of cake. Sweetened mascarpone is equally sturdy, as is very stiffly beaten whipped cream stabilized with confectioners' sugar or vanilla pudding.

pastry flour *See* flour.

pâté (*pah-tay*) This classic French dish can be made from meats, poultry, fish, or vegetables and be ground anywhere from coarse to a purée and then cooked. Pâté is usually bound with eggs to hold it together, and it's served as a first course. If baked in a mold, it's called a *terrine*. For coarse-textured pâté, meatloaf is an alternative. For soft and finely textured fish dishes, use commercial spreads such as smoked bluefish dip or smoked salmon and cream cheese spread.

pattypan squash A member of the summer squash family, the pattypan looks like a round cushion with a scalloped edge. They're light green when young and almost white when larger. Either zucchini or yellow squash have a similar flavor and texture.

peach Peaches come in two kinds: freestone and clingstone. Clingstone flesh must be cut away from the stone. But there's no difference in flavor between the two. The best substitute for cooking are nectarines in most cases. For a fruit salad, mango and papaya also add an orange color to the mix.

peanut Peanuts are actually a member of the legume family rather than a nut that comes off a tree, but we eat them as nuts. The distinctive flavor is hard to replicate, but walnuts and pecans can be used in the same way.

peanut butter   We most often see sweetened peanut butter, but natural peanut butter is merely peanuts and peanut oil ground to a paste. Almond butter and cashew butter are available in most whole foods markets and health food stores, and they're the best choice to avoid a possible peanut allergy. It's easy to make it yourself, too.

Yield: 1 cup

1 ½ cups salted cocktail
   peanuts (not dry roasted)
⅓ cup peanut oil

Granulated sugar or honey to
   taste (optional)

Place peanuts in a food processor fitted with a steel blade and purée until smooth. Slowly add oil through the feed tube until mixture forms a paste. Add sugar, if using, and process until smooth. For chunky peanut butter, reserve ¼ cup peanuts and add them at the end of processing, chopping them using on-and-off pulsing action. Store refrigerated for up to 1 week.

---

peanut oil   *See* fats and oils.

pear   One of the fruits that bridges the season from summer into fall and winter, pears are sweet, juicy, and buttery and can be enjoyed in a number of ways. They retain their shape when baked or poached and can be used for sauces and tarts. Here are the various varieties you'll find:

Anjou   Light green or yellow green, and almost egg-shaped with little definition of a shoulder and a short stem, Anjous are thin-skinned with a smooth texture. Anjous are good eating pears. When ripe, the flavor is sweet, spicy, and very juicy. The Anjou is the most abundant of all fresh varieties.

Bartlett   A bell-shape pear, Bartletts are considered a summer fruit because they're most available in July, but they're also available into late fall. The flesh is white, smooth, and juicy with an excellent flavor for fresh eating and salads. Bartletts hold their shape well in baking, poaching, and canning.

Bosc   Distinguished by its symmetrical body, the Bosc has a long, tapered neck and slim stem. When ripe, it has a golden brown skin and russeting over the golden yellow. The flesh is tender, buttery, and aromatic.

Comice   With a wonderful chubby shape and a short neck and stem, the Comice has a tendency to turn from green to greenish yellow, and frequently has a crimson blush. Its eating quality is superb, and its flesh is very smooth, aromatic, and extremely juicy with a particularly sweet flavor.

Seckel   The smallest of all pear varieties, the Seckel can be green with dark red blush or nearly all red. As the Seckel ripens, the red becomes brighter and the green takes on a yellow hue. The flesh is a warm ivory color and tastes very sweet.

Any variety of pears can be substituted for one another in a recipe. Apples can be substituted for pears, but the cooking time needs to be lengthened and more sugar is required because pears are inherently sweeter than apples.

pearl barley   *See* barley.

pearl onion   *See* onion.

pecan   This American nut grown in the temperate climate of the southern states is known for richness and has the highest oil content of any nut. The flavor is distinctive, but walnuts and hazelnuts are the closest in level of intensity.

pecorino   *See* cheese.

penne   *See* pasta, dried.

pepita (*pay-PEA-tahs*)   *See* pumpkin seed.

peppercorn   From east to west, pepper is appreciated for its warm aroma and spicy flavor. It stimulates the taste buds to appreciate the other flavors in a dish, as well as adding its own flavor. Here are the most familiar forms of peppercorn:

black   These are the unripe berries that have been left to dry and darken. Pepper steak relies on black pepper as the primary seasoning; a crust of crushed peppercorns are pounded into the meat before grilling.

green   These are the unripe pepper berries that are not dried. They share the same basic taste of dried peppercorns, but they also have a sharp, almost acidic flavor that makes them useful as a foil to rich meats such as duck or as a contrast to delicate foods such as fish. Green peppercorns are preserved in brine, so always rinse the berries before use.

pink   These are the berries of a small South American shrub. With a slightly piquant taste, pink peppercorns are a decorative alternative to green peppercorns, or the two may be used in combination. Use sparingly, however, because pink peppercorns can be toxic in great quantity of 1 teaspoon or more.

Szechwan   Known also as *fagara* or *anise-pepper,* these are the dried berries of an Asian shrub or small tree and are more aromatic than Western peppercorns. To release the fragrance, toast Szechwan peppercorns in a dry skillet, grind them in a food processor, and then strain them to separate the pepper from the woody husk.

white   These are the same berries as the black peppercorns, but ripened, dried, and with the outer casings removed. The result is a less aromatic heat. White pepper is usually reserved for creamy recipes in which specks of black would be unattractive.

Black and white peppercorns can be substituted for one another in direct proportion. For green peppercorns in brine, nonpareil capers are the best alternative. There's really no substitute for Szechwan pepper, but if you use black pepper to supply heat, use only ½ the amount.

peppermint   *See* mint.

pepperoncini (*pep-per-ahn-CHEE-knee*)   *See* chilies, fresh.

pepperoni   Used most often as a pizza topping, this firm Italian sausage is most similar to hard salami and soppressata, either of which can be substituted.

pequín chili (*pay-KEEN*)   *See* chilies, dried.

perch   A freshwater fish, perch is sometimes called walleyed pike, although it's not a member of the pike family. Whitefish is the best substitute; it has the same white flesh and sweet flavor.

perilla (*pur-illa*)   *See* shiso.

Pernod (*pear-noh*)   *See* liqueur, anise.

Persian melon   *See* melon.

persimmon   There are actually two main varieties of persimmon, one of the few brightly colored fall and winter fruit. The Fuyu has a somewhat flattened shape and crisp texture, and the Hachiya is the more common. The latter is larger and oblong with a pointed end, and it's the best for baking. Apples can be substituted for Fuyu, while a purée of mango or peach is the best stand-in for Hachiya, with a bit of lemon or lime juice added to give these sweeter fruits an acidic component.

pesto   This uncooked basil sauce is closely associated with the Genoa area of Italy, but its name really means "pounded" in Italian. It's available in the refrigerated section of most supermarkets, or you can easily make it yourself.

Yield: 1 cup

¼ cup pine nuts
2 cups firmly packed fresh
  basil leaves
4 garlic cloves, peeled
⅓ cup extra-virgin olive oil

½ cup freshly grated
  Parmesan cheese
Salt and freshly ground black
  pepper

Preheat the oven to 350°F. Place pine nuts in a small pan and toast in the oven for 5 to 7 minutes or until lightly browned. Set aside. Combine basil, garlic, and pine nuts in a food processor fitted with a steel blade, and process until basil and garlic are finely chopped. Pour olive oil slowly through the feed tube and then scrape the sides of the work bowl. Add cheese and process until combined. Season with salt and pepper. If you're not using pesto immediately, scrape it into a container and float a few tablespoons of olive oil on top to keep basil bright green. Pesto can be refrigerated for up to 4 days, tightly covered, but the flavor fades after a few hours.

Petite Syrah (*peh-teet sear-ah*)   *See* wine, red.

petrale sole   This fish caught in the Pacific from Alaska to California is really a member of the flounder family. Flounder or English sole are the best substitutes.

pheasant   *See* game bird.

phyllo (or **filo**) (*FEE-low*)   These almost paper thin sheets of pastry are used for both sweet and savory Greek and Middle Eastern dishes and must be handled very carefully to prevent breaking. Asian rice paper pancakes and European strudel dough are the best alternatives. You can also use French puff pastry, but roll it out as thin as possible first.

pickerel   *See* pike.

pickling spices   This potent blend of flavorful and aromatic herbs and spices is used as a preservative as well as a seasoning. Crab boil and Old Bay seasoning have many of the same ingredients.

picnic shoulder   *See* pork.

pignoli (*peen-YOH-lee*)   *See* pine nut.

pike   The flesh of this freshwater fish is flaky and very lean, and small pike are usually sold as pickerel. Whitefish is the best substitute.

pimiento   Pimiento, a variation on roasted red bell pepper, is often used as the stuffing for green olives. You can either roast the pepper yourself or purchase it jarred.

pine nut   These tiny seeds painstakingly extracted from certain pinecones are used extensively in Italian and Mexican cuisine. They have a mild flavor, so cashews or macadamia nuts are your best alternatives.

pineapple   No fruit really has the same sunny yellow color and succulent flavor as the pineapple. Canned pineapple packed in its juice is the best substitute for fresh if you can't find a ripe one. If you don't mind giving up the yellow color, use mango or papaya.

pink peppercorn   *See* peppercorn.

piñon (*PEEN-yon*)   *See* pine nut.

Pinot Blanc (*pee-noh blahnc*)   *See* wine, white.

Pinot Grigio (*pee-noh GREE-joh*)   *See* wine, white.

Pinot Noir (*pee-noh nwahr*)   *See* wine, red.

pinto bean (*PEEN-toh*) *See* beans, dried.

pistachio nut It's easy to know when a pistachio nut is ready to eat—the shell splits so it's easy to open. No nuts share the same attractive pale green color, but both pine nuts and hazelnuts have a similar sweet flavor.

pita bread Sometimes called "pocket bread," pita is the round Middle Eastern flatbread that's cut horizontally to form a pouch. Flour tortillas and Armenian lavash flatbread can be used in place of pita bread, but you'll have to wrap rather than stuff the fillings.

plantain (*PLAN-tihn*) These large cousins of the common banana are used as potatoes in Latin American and Caribbean cooking; they're fried and boiled either ripe or while green when they still have a mild flavor. Substitute green bananas or sweet potatoes for green plantains; try ripe bananas for black plantains, the color they become when they're ripe.

plum Perhaps more than most fruits, plums vary in their shape, color, and flavor. Available from May through late September, plums range from tart and acidic to very sweet; select plums according to their intended use. A short season plum, the sweet Italian one, is perhaps the most succulent. More than 150 varieties of plum are grown in North America, and their characteristics vary widely. The following table offers a look at the major varieties.

Plums at a Glance

Plum	Characteristics
Damson	dark skin and flesh, used only for preserves
Friar	dark-red skin, deep-yellow flesh
Greengage	green-yellow skin, yellow flesh
Italian prune	small, oval, with blue-purple skin and firm golden flesh
Laroda	large, with yellow skin and flesh
Red Beauty	bright red skin, firm yellow flesh
Santa Rosa	very tart, purple skin, and yellow flesh

Many plum varieties can be substituted for one another. You can also substitute a combination of pears with hydrated prunes to achieve a similar flavor to fresh plums, although the color will be decidedly different—a rather unattractive brown.

plum sauce   This more sweet than sour Chinese condiment is used as a dipping sauce and spread on thin pancakes when eating moo shu dishes or Peking duck. Mango chutney has the same fruit flavor but it's spicier; purée the chutney so it has the same smooth consistency.

plum tomato   *See* tomato.

poblano chili (*poh-BLAN-oh*)   *See* chilies, fresh.

Poilly-Fuissé (*poiyee fwesay*)   *See* wine, white.

polenta (*poh-LEHN-tah*)   *See* cornmeal.

Polish sausage   *See* kielbasa.

pollock   *See* cod.

pomegranate   This richly colored fall fruit, about the size of an apple, has hard, leatherlike skin; the juice is in tiny capsules surrounding individual seeds. The juice from blood oranges is about the only substitute to give you the same tantalizing taste, although cranberry juice does have the same color.

pomelo   The pomelo looks like a pear-shape grapefruit with a green or yellow rind. They're grown only for their thick rind, which is candied and sold as citron. Candied lemon peel or grapefruit peel is your best bet.

pompano   This famous fish from the Florida coast has smooth skin and does not need scaling. Grouper and red snapper both have the same firm flesh and mild, almost sweet flavor.

ponzu sauce (*pon-zoo*)   A salty and sour Japanese condiment, ponzu sauce is often served as a dipping sauce for shashimi. Japanese soy sauce is the major ingredient, so it can be used as an alternative.

poppy seed   Poppy seeds are the mature seeds of the beautiful flower that also produces opium; the seeds are so tiny, it takes abut 900,000 seeds to produce a single pound. Their slate-black color makes them a popular topping for breads and other baked goods. Black sesame seeds are about the only alternative.

porcini (*por-CHEE-knee*)   *See* mushroom, wild.

porgy   There are many varieties of this fish; scup is the most popular and plentiful. Porgies are known for the sweetness of their lean and flaky flesh. Your best substitutes are red snapper and rockfish.

pork   Be it a succulent down-home barbecued sparerib or an elegant crown roast, pork is one of the most delicious, finely textured meats available, and its delicate flavor makes it adaptable to a wide range of seasonings, marinades, and sauces.

All cuts of pork are relatively tender, and there's no official grading system as there is for beef. As of 1986, the U.S. Department of Agriculture stopped inspecting fresh pork for *Trichinella spiralis*, and although pork is cooked to a higher internal temperature than beef and lamb, there's no longer a need to cook it to 180°F, at which time it goes beyond well done to dried out.

The following table gives you choices for cuts of pork, but either turkey or chicken are alternatives for almost all pork recipes, with the exception of a crown roast. You can use chicken on the bone either with or without skin as a substitute for pork chops, and a boneless breast or thigh for a boneless chop. For a loin roast, a boned and tied turkey breast is an option, too.

Pork at a Glance

Pork	Origin	Cooking Method(s)
Arm chops	shoulder	braise, broil
Arm roast	shoulder	braise, roast
Blade chops	loin	braise
Boston butt	shoulder	braise, roast
Country ribs	loin	braise, grill
Loin chop	loin	broil, stuff, grill
Loin roast	loin	roast
Picnic shoulder	shoulder	roast, braise

continues

Pork at a Glance   (continued)

Pork	Origin	Cooking Method(s)
Rib chop	center loin	broil, grill, braise
Sirloin chop	center loin	broil, stuff, grill
Spareribs	loin	broil, grill
Tenderloin	loin	roast, grill

What to do when cooking pork and you change from boneless cuts to those with bones? The following table helps you determine how much you'll need.

Pork per Person

Cut	With Bone	Without Bone
Chop	12 oz.	8 oz.
Country ribs	12 oz.	8 oz.
Roast	10 to 12 oz.	6 to 8 oz.
Spareribs	1½ lb.	n/a
Tenderloin	n/a	6 to 8 oz.

pork, ground   Ground veal and ground turkey are good substitutes for ground pork. Beef or lamb are too strongly flavored and the wrong color.

Port   *See* wine, fortified.

porterhouse steak   *See* beef.

portobello (*port-oh-BELL-oh*)   *See* mushroom, wild.

Port-Salut (*por sah-loo*)   *See* cheese.

pot cheese   This fresh cheese is essentially cottage cheese that's been allowed to drain so it becomes firmer and drier. To duplicate it, place cottage cheese in a strainer over a mixing bowl for 1 hour, refrigerated. Or substitute ricotta cheese drained in the same way.

potato   Potatoes are tubers, the swellings of the root of the plant. That's the key to their nutritious qualities—the valuable nutrients of the plant are stored in the roots.

all-purpose   All-purpose potatoes—new, round red, baby, or white—can be either baked or boiled and are generally white or red.

bakers   Bakers—Idaho and russets—have more starch and can be described as mealy or floury. They are light and fluffy when cooked. In addition to baking, they're wonderful for mashing and for french fries.

boilers   Boilers—Finnish and Yukon gold—have less starch but more moisture. They have thin skin, yet hold their shape quite well when sliced. They're perfect for potato salad and for sautéing.

Potatoes at a Glance

Potato	Color	Uses
Baby	varies	steamed, grilled
Finnish	yellow	steamed, boiled
Idaho	brown	baked, mashed, fried
New	red	steamed, boiled, salad
Round red	red	steamed, boiled, salad
Russet	brown	baked, mashed, fried
White	white	steamed, boiled, baked, fried
Yukon gold	yellow	steamed, boiled

P

Toque Tips

Baked potatoes can be reheated without overcooking by dipping them in cold water and then putting them into a 350°F oven for 10 minutes. The water potatoes are boiled in can be saved for soup or gravy. Adding vinegar to the salted water when boiling potatoes for potato salad keeps the potatoes from falling apart.

potato chips   Called *crisps* in other English-speaking countries, tortilla chips or pretzels give you the same crispy texture. Or make them yourself by slicing potatoes into paper-thin slices. Fry them in vegetable oil heated to 375°F for 2 minutes, or until crisp and brown. Drain on paper towels.

potato starch   Used as a thickening agent, potato starch can be used interchangeably with cornstarch.

poultry seasoning   This traditional herb blend is sold most often around Thanksgiving, although it's great with all poultry—from baby poussin to groaning board turkeys.

Yield: ⅓ *cup*

2 TB. dried marjoram
2 TB. dried savory
2 TB. rubbed dried sage

1 TB. dried thyme
2 tsp. dried rosemary

Combine marjoram, savory, sage, thyme, and rosemary in a small bowl. Store in an airtight jar for up to 6 months.

---

poussin (*poo-sahn*)   *See* chicken.

praline   Essentially, praline is some sort of toasted nut—pecans in the South for sure—that's mixed with caramelized sugar and either eaten as candy or crushed as an ingredient for baked goods. Peanut brittle or any nut brittle is the same thing and can be used interchangeably.

prawn   *See* shrimp.

preserves   The basic difference between preserves and jam is the size of the pieces of fruit; those in preserves are larger. A jam of the same flavor can always be used in place of preserves. Jelly delivers the same flavor, but usually doesn't contain the bits of fruit preserves have.

pretzel   This German-born quintessential American snack comes either soft and doughy or crisp and hard. Bagels are the best alternative for soft pretzels, and they come salt-coated as well. For crisp pretzels, the sky's the limit: potato chips, tortilla chips, bagel chips, pita crisps, or any wheat cracker work.

prickly pear   This is actually the fruit from the Nopal cactus, which is prized in Southwest cooking for its leaves. Prickly pears have a sweet, watermelonlike flavor and a blushing color. They can be used for soufflés and mousses as well as for jams and fruit salads. Watermelon is your best substitution.

Food Foibles

Always handle prickly pears with tongs because the prickles are hard to detect. Should you get one embedded in your skin, remove it with tweezers or tape.

prime rib   *See* beef.

prosciutto (*pro-SHOO-toh*)   *See* ham.

provolone (*proh-voh-LOH-neh*)   *See* cheese.

prune   A prune is simply a sun-ripened Italian plum; both are used for savory and sweet dishes. It takes about 3 pounds plums to make 1 pound prunes. Dried figs and dried dates make good substitutions for prunes; many figs are almost the same size, too.

puff pastry   Puff pastry is one of the hardest things I've ever had to make. The process involves rolling sheets of butter between layers of dough, and the butter melting and creating steam pushes the layers apart as they bake. Sheets of phyllo dough brushed with melted butter create the same crispness as puff pastry, and if puff pastry is to be used as a piecrust, just use a basic piecrust.

P

pumpernickel   This dense, dark bread has a high percentage of rye flour, so a dark rye bread made without caraway seeds is your best alternative choice.

pumpkin   This American winter squash is synonymous with Thanksgiving pies, but it's really quite versatile for all baked goods as well as soups and purées. For pies, solid-pack canned pumpkin can be used, but don't use pumpkin pie filling because it already contains spices and liquid. For other cooking, acorn, hubbard, and butternut squash are good alternatives.

pumpkin pie spice   This blending of aromatic spices includes all those listed separately in most recipes, with cinnamon as the dominant one. In a pinch, you can always use cinnamon; apple pie spice is a similar mix but doesn't contain ginger.

1 TB. apple pie spice = 1^1/$_2$ tsp. ground cinnamon + ^{1}/$_2$ tsp. ground ginger + ^{1}/$_2$ tsp. ground nutmeg + ^{1}/$_4$ tsp. ground cloves + ^{1}/$_4$ tsp. ground allspice

pumpkin seed   After they're rinsed and baked, pumpkin seeds become a healthful snack and can also be used to decorate the tops of baked goods. Sunflower seeds are similar in taste and texture.

quahog   *See* clam.

quail   *See* game bird.

quail egg   These delicacies are sold in many gourmet markets. One large chicken egg equals four quail eggs in volume.

quatre épices (*cah-trah a-piece*)   This aromatic spice blend of nutmeg, ginger, cloves, and pepper is used in many classic French meat dishes. Use pumpkin pie spice or apple pie spice in the same amount, and add ¼ teaspoon freshly ground white pepper for each 1 teaspoon of spice blend. Chinese five-spice powder has a similar flavor.

queso fresco (*KAY-soh FRESS-koh*)   This fresh Mexican cheese tastes like a slightly salty cottage or pot cheese, both of which can be substituted. Be sure to add a bit more salt to the recipe when using the substitutes.

quince   Quince resembles a golden apple or yellow pear, and has a taste related to both, but it must be cooked to be enjoyed. Once it's cooked, the flesh turns a blushing pink; the strong, astringent taste becomes mellow; and the hard pebbly texture turns smooth. It's most frequently made into quince sauce, and to replicate the flavor use a proportion of ⅔ apples with red skin and ⅓ pears for the quince in your recipe. After it's strained, the sauce will have the same pink color as quince sauce. For baking, substitute a good baking apple like a Jonathan or Rome Beauty; it takes about the same amount of time to bake.

Toque Tips

Quince is a delicious fruit to use for preserves. It contains a high percentage of natural pectin so the preserves gel naturally without the addition of pectin.

quinoa (*KEEN-wah*)   Quinoa resembles rice and cooks in about half the time. Its flavor is delicate, and it has a slightly crunchy texture. What to substitute for this grain varies because quinoa comes in colors ranging from pale tan to red to almost black-brown. For the light shades, couscous is the best alternative. Buckwheat groats, bulgur, or millet are good substitutions for the darker colors.

Q

R

rabbit   Domestic rabbit is almost indistinguishable from chicken; it has the same color, flavor, and texture. So chicken is an obvious alternative. But the same cannot be said for hare; the wild version usually is only available via mail-order sources. Goose or duck is a passable alternative to hare, but the meat of both contains far more fat.

raclette (*rah-klett*)   *See* cheese.

radiatore (*rah-dee-ah-TOH-ray*)   *See* pasta, dried.

radicchio (*rah-DEE-k'yoh*)   *See* lettuce.

radish   This smallest of all the root vegetables has a crisp texture and a sharp, peppery flavor. We most often associate radishes as being red, but they are also white and lavender, and can be either round or oblong in shape. Black radishes have an even stronger flavor, similar to that of horseradish. Daikon, a Japanese radish, can be substituted for Western radishes, and in salads, you can use a sharp pungent green such as mustard greens or kale.

rainbow trout   *See* trout.

raisin   Grapes have been dried in the sun and transformed into raisins since biblical times and are used in both savory and sweet dishes. Here are the main types you'll find:

>   *golden seedless*   Made from the Thompson seedless, golden seedless raisins are oven-dried to maintain their light, natural color. This results in a tarter flavor, which works well in baking.

Muscat   These highly regarded raisins are sun-dried Muscat of Alexandria grapes. The seeds are mechanically removed, and the raisins are quite large and dark. They have a rich, sweet flavor.

natural seedless   These well-known, dark raisins are also sun-dried from Thompson seedless grapes. They're primarily used in cooking and eating out of hand.

sultana   These are similar in color to regular raisins, but the flavor is slightly tarter. They are frequently specified in European cookbooks. You can sub regular raisins.

zante currant   These sun-dried Black Corinth grapes have no relation to currants. These raisins are very small, seedless, and have a delightful, unique, more interesting sweet-tart flavor.

Any type of raisin can be substituted for another with the exception of zante currants, which have a tangier flavor. You can use chopped dates in place of raisins, and a combination of raisins and finely chopped dried apricots are a good substitute for zante currants.

Toque Tips

Some baking recipes call for chopping raisins because it distributes them more evenly in the batter or dough. To ease chopping, toss 1 cup raisins with 1 teaspoon vegetable oil and then chop with a sharp knife or with on-and-off pulsing action in a food processor fitted with a steel blade. Adding a bit of the flour specified in the recipe helps chopping, too.

R

ramen   This wheat-based egg noodle is very popular in Japan. Any thin egg noodle can be used in its place.

ramps   These wild leeks grow all along the Appalachian Trail, and they look like small leeks but have a garlic flavor note. Leeks or Chinese chives are your best alternatives.

rapini (*rah-PEE-neh*)   *See* greens.

ras el hanout (*raas el hahn-OUT*)   This complex spice blend used in Moroccan cooking contains a long list of components. Garam masala has many of the same ingredients.

raspberry   Each raspberry actually consists of many fruits because each tiny section has a small, hard seed. Today, in addition to traditional red and black raspberries, you'll find golden ones. Strawberries or blackberries are your best substitute for fresh dishes, and frozen, *dry-packed* raspberries can be used in fruit sauces.

Sub-Text

Dry-packed foods are individually frozen and then placed in a bag. Almost all vegetables are dry-packed, but most fruits come both in that condition and frozen in a sugar syrup.

ravioli (*rah-vee-OH-lee*)   *See* pasta, stuffed.

red bean   *See* beans, dried.

Red Beauty plum   *See* plum.

red cabbage   *See* cabbage.

red onion   *See* onion.

red pepper   *See* cayenne.

red pepper, roasted   *See* pimiento.

red snapper   The flesh of this fish found most often in the Gulf of Mexico is heralded as simultaneously firm and tender with an innate moisture and sweet flavor. The skin is almost always left on the fillets. Black sea bass, grouper, and striped bass are the best alternatives.

red wine vinegar   *See* vinegar.

redfish   *See* drum.

reindeer   *See* game meat.

retsina   *See* wine, white.

rhubarb   Called the "pie plant" and botanically a vegetable, the pink stalks of rhubarb are cooked as a dessert. Rhubarb is never eaten raw, and it takes a lot of sugar to reach even a sweet-tart flavor profile. No ingredient gives rhubarb's blushing pink color, but using pineapple (without additional sugar) in a pie gives it the same sweet-tart flavor.

rib-eye steak *See* beef.

Ricard (*ree-card*) *See* liqueur.

rice All 2,500 species of rice, the world's most popular grain, trace their lineage to India. When rice comes from the field, it's termed *paddy rice* and must have the nonedible hull removed before it can be eaten. Brown rice is whole or broken kernels of rice from which only the hull has been removed. Grains of white rice are rubbed together to remove this natural bran.

Rice is classified primarily by the size of the grain. Long grains are five times longer than they are wide, and when cooked, the grains tend to remain separate. Medium grains are plump but not round, and when cooked, medium-grain rice tends to be more moist and tender than long grain. Used for sushi and other Japanese dishes, short-grain rice is almost round in shape, and tends to cling together when cooked, which is why it's sometimes called sticky rice.

There's a whole world of rice out there; here's a guide to the popular varieties:

arborio This medium-grain rice is primarily imported from Italy and used for risotto. When liquid is slowly added while the rice is stirred constantly, the resulting risotto is creamy from the slow release of starch and the rice is still firm to the bite. Carnaroli and vialone nano also work well for risotto.

basmati The name of this rice means "queen of fragrance," and it's the best known of the aromatic rices. The nutlike aroma results from a high concentration of acetyl pyroline, a compound naturally found in all rice. A similar species is now being raised in the United States and marketed under the name Tex-Mati. Jasmine rice is the best substitute for a fragrant bowl.

brown This is unmilled rice with the hulls removed. It can be long, medium, or short grain, depending on the species harvested, and it requires a longer cooking time than white rice to sufficiently cook the husk. While white rice can be used in its place, it won't have the same nutty flavor. Try grains such as bulgur and buckwheat groats.

converted Converted rice is steamed before it's husked, which lets the grains absorb many of the nutrients housed in the husk. When it's cooked, the grains are more nutritious and firmer than those of white long-grain rice. Any long-grain brown or white rice can be used in place of converted rice.

glutinous   This short-grain rice, used primarily in Asia, is very sticky, although it doesn't contain any gluten. Arborio or short-grain white rice are the best alternatives.

Himalayan red   The difference between this rice and long-grain brown rice is the color of the bran—red, not brown. Brown rice tastes almost identical but doesn't have the same lovely color.

jasmine   Also called Thai basmati rice, this fragrant rice has an almost floral aroma, and it's sold both as white and brown rice. Use basmati or medium-grain white rice in its place.

Toque Tips

If the rice at the bottom of the pot is cooked and at the top of the pot is raw, too much steam is escaping. Give the rice a big stir, cover the pot either with foil or with a tea towel (be sure to fold the loose ends up over the top), replace the lid, and continue cooking.

rice cracker   These crispy crackers made from rice flour are essentially bland, but they're also sold flavored with everything from tamari to seaweed. Any water cracker made from wheat is a good substitute.

rice paper   These circular sheets made from a paste of rice flour are extremely brittle and have to be soaked in water before they can be used. Phyllo is about the only other food that's as thin and creates a crispy wrapper when fried or baked.

rice vinegar   *See* vinegar.

ricotta (*ree-KOH-tah*)   This fresh Italian cheese with a granular yet creamy texture is frequently made from the whey resulting from making fresh mozzarella. Farmer's cheese and pot cheese are the best substitutions, although they're a bit more sour so you might want to add a few tablespoons sugar.

Riesling (*REEZ-ling*)   *See* wine, white.

rigatoni (*ree-gah-TONE-eh*)   *See* pasta, dried.

Rioja (*ree-OH-ha*)   *See* wine, red.

riso (*REE-soh*)   *See* pasta, dried.

risotto (*ree-SOH-tow*)   This classic Italian rice dish hails from Milan, Italy, and is laboriously made by stirring arborio rice while slowly adding stock to encourage the starch to leach out. You can cook any medium-grain rice in stock and then add a few tablespoons Parmesan cheese at the end to replicate the flavor.

Rock Cornish hen   *See* chicken.

rock lobster   Also called spiny lobster, these warm-water crustaceans have a nice large tail but no claws to speak of. You can use Maine lobster tails in its place, but the flavor of rock lobster is not as sweet; it's really more akin to giant prawns.

rock salt   *See* salt.

rocket   *See* lettuce.

rockfish   Although striped bass is often identified incorrectly as rockfish, authentic rockfish are a large family of species in the Pacific Ocean, most of which have very firm flesh and a mild flavor. Halibut and turbot are the best substitutes.

rolled oats   *See* oat.

romaine   *See* lettuce.

Romano (*roh-MAH-noh*)   *See* cheese.

Roquefort (*roke-fhort*)   *See* cheese.

rosemary   The herb rosemary really suffers from being used in a dried form; it lacks almost all the aroma you get with the fresh version. In a pinch, use 1 teaspoon dried rosemary for each 1 tablespoon fresh, but add 1 tablespoon chopped fresh parsley, too. Or use fresh oregano or fresh basil; the flavor is different but adds hints of evergreen and citrus.

rotelle (*roh-TELL-ahy*)   *See* pasta, dried.

rotini (*row-TEE-knee*)   *See* pasta, dried.

rouille (*roo-ee*)   This garlicky sauce is akin to the famous aioli from Provence. It can quickly be made at home.

Yield: ¼ *cup*

¼ cup mayonnaise
2 TB. pimiento or roasted red
  bell pepper
3 garlic cloves, peeled and
  minced

1 TB. freshly squeezed lemon
  juice
Salt and pepper

Combine mayonnaise, pimiento, garlic, and lemon juice in a food
processor fitted with a steel blade or in a blender. Purée until smooth,
and season with salt and pepper. Refrigerate for up to 4 days, tightly
covered.

roux (*roo*)   This paste of flour cooked in some sort of fat—either butter
or oil—is used as a thickening agent for soups and sauces. To substitute,
use 1 tablespoon cornstarch mixed with 2 tablespoons cold water for
each 2 tablespoons of roux specified in a recipe. Or use a mixture of
1 tablespoon unsalted butter, softened, mixed with 1 tablespoon all-
purpose flour for each 2 tablespoons roux called for.

rum   *See* spirits.

rum extract   This gives food the flavor of rum without adding alcohol.
If you don't care about adding the alcoholic content (most of which
burns off anyway if a dish is cooked), substitute 3 tablespoons rum
for each 1 teaspoon rum extract, and subtract liquid from the recipe
accordingly.

rump roast   *See* beef.

Russian dressing (or **Thousand Island dressing**)   This flavored,
mayonnaise-based salad dressing can also be used as a topping sauce for
grilled seafood or poultry.

Yield: 2 cups

1 ½ cups mayonnaise
¼ cup ketchup
¼ cup sweet pickle relish

1 shallot, peeled and
  chopped
1 tsp. white horseradish
Hot red pepper sauce

Stir together mayonnaise, ketchup, sweet pickle relish, shallot,
horseradish, and hot red pepper sauce. Refrigerate for up to 4 days,
tightly covered.

---

rutabaga   People often confuse rutabagas with giant turnips because
they have the same variegated purple and light yellow skin. But this
golden-fleshed vegetable, invented in the seventeenth century, has
the earthy flavor of its parents—turnips and cabbage. Turnips can be
substituted, but their flavor is sweeter. For a purée, use 3 parts turnip
to 1 part green cabbage. For roasted vegetables, you can also use Yukon
gold potatoes to achieve the golden color of rutabagas.

rye bread   This dense bread made from primarily rye flour is often
flavored with caraway seeds. Pumpernickel or a dense herb bread are
your best choices, although I can't see a corned beef sandwich going on
anything but rye bread!

rye whisky   *See* spirits.

R

safflower oil   *See* fats and oils.

saffron   If you want to win a trivia contest, remember that saffron—the three stigmas from a species of crocus plant—is the most expensive food in the world. It imparts an orange-yellow color and slightly pungent flavor to foods. Turmeric gives the same color, although the flavor is different.

¼ tsp. crushed saffron threads = 1 tsp. turmeric

sage   This member of the mint family gives foods a musky flavor with a slightly hot aftertaste. You'll find two forms of dried sage on the market. Rubbed sage delivers almost the same flavor; ground sage turns food an unappealing olive green color without lending much flavor in the process.

1 TB. chopped fresh sage = 2 tsp. rubbed sage

Saint André (*sah ahn-dray*)   *See* cheese.

sake (*sah-key*)   In addition to being a beverage of choice with Japanese food, this rice wine is also an ingredient used in many dishes. Although made from grapes, not rice, both dry vermouth and dry sherry have a similar flavor.

salami   *Salami* is a generic term for many forms of Italian pork-based sausage, most of which include garlic and pepper; there's also a kosher salami made only with beef. In the Italian family, pepperoni and sopressata are good substitutions. Spanish chorizo or Portuguese linguiça are also viable alternatives.

salmon   A very popular fish because of its rich, buttery taste and blushing pink-orange flesh, salmon can be wild or farmed. Here are the most common species:

chinook   The largest salmon, chinooks weigh between 10 and 20 pounds (although they can weigh more than 100 pounds) and are considered the finest eating salmon. The large flakes of the soft flesh are very flavorful with a pinkish-white to red color.

chum   This salmon is coarse-textured and is the lowest in fat. It has orange-pink roe with large juicy eggs often referred to as "salmon caviar," which is salted and treated as sturgeon eggs.

coho   Also called silver salmon, cohos are smaller, averaging 6 to 12 pounds. Fine in texture, the flesh is relatively lean and has a bright red color. Baby cohos are particularly tasty.

pink   The smallest of the salmons, weighing only about 3 pounds, pink salmon are peach in color with small flakes and very little fat.

sockeye   This fish has deep orange-red flesh and is often also called red salmon. Weighing 4 to 6 pounds, it has a rich flavor and firm, small-flaked flesh.

Unfortunately, no species of fish have the same color as salmon, but many species can be cooked the same way. For salmon fillets, substitute striped bass, red snapper, or bluefish. For salmon steaks, tuna, swordfish, and halibut are your best options.

salmon, smoked   Usually made from larger fish with meatier sides, salmon is smoked in a number of countries, including Scotland, Norway, and the United States. The flavor of the smoking depends on the type of wood used, and the intensity is determined by its length of smoking. These are all cold-smoking methods, during which smoke is blown into a chamber by a fan, thus curing the fish very slowly. As is true for fresh salmon, no other smoked fish has the same orange color, but both smoked bluefish and smoked whitefish have similar high oil contents.

salsify   This root vegetable, also called oyster plant, is not as sweet as a parsnip but looks like a larger version of one. Jerusalem artichokes and parsnips are your best alternatives.

S

salt One of the four basic flavors discernible by the human taste buds, salt is necessary to create a background in foods in which other flavors can be detected; that's why at least a pinch of salt is added to all sweet baked goods. You can find various forms of salt on the market, but they cannot all be substituted for one another in equal amounts because their granular formation and flavors vary.

kosher Also known as "coarse salt" or "pickling salt," this purified rock salt is coarsely ground and does not contain magnesium carbonate. As with sea salt, it's preferred by cooks.

rock This unrefined coarse salt is not added directly to foods but is used in some ice cream machines and as a base for baked clams and oysters.

sea Sea salt is made by allowing sea water to evaporate. This is the type of salt preferred by cooks because of its purity and lack of chemicals.

table Table salt is finely ground rock salt. Most of what's on the market is fortified with iodine and treated with magnesium carbonate to prevent clumping, but it can also produce a metallic flavor.

Here are some formulas for substituting salt:

1 tsp. table salt = 1½ TB. kosher salt or 2 tsp. ground sea salt

2 TB. crystal sea salt = 1 TB. ground sea salt

Toque Tips

It's always best to use only a sprinkling of salt at the beginning of cooking a dish and wait until it's ready to serve to season it to the level you want. As the food cooks and the liquid evaporates, dishes tend to get too salty.

salt cod Prior to refrigeration, salting and drying foods was a primary method of preservation. Salt cod, or any dried salted fish, should always be soaked before using it. The best substitute for salt cod is anchovy paste, used at the rate of 1 teaspoon anchovy paste per 1 ounce salt cod.

salt pork *See* bacon.

Sambuca (*sam-BOO-kuh*) *See* liqueur.

Sangiovese (*san-jo-VEH-see*)   *See* wine, red.

Santa Claus melon   *See* melon.

Santa Rosa plum   *See* plum.

Sap Sago (*sahp sahgo*)   *See* cheese.

sardine   The name *sardine* is used for any tiny saltwater fish with soft bones such as tiny herring or anchovies. Sardines in the United States are always canned, either in oil or in tomato sauce. Most sardines are sold whole, and small, canned herring is the best substitution. Other times, you'll find them sold as boned fillets; anchovy fillets are the best alternative in this case.

sauerkraut   The German word *sauerkraut* literally means "sour cabbage," and the dish is made by fermenting salted cabbage. Korean kim chee is a similar food, although it contains a lot of hot pepper. A Chinese dish called *suan cai*, which means "sour vegetable," works, too. Another choice is sour pickles, which are made with the same process.

sausage   There's a whole spectrum of cooked and smoked sausages; fresh sausage is merely ground meat that's been seasoned. It's then stuffed into casings to form links or used in bulk. Substitute ground pork for pork sausage and ground beef for beef sausage, and adjust the seasonings accordingly. For example, Italian sausage is flavored with garlic and fennel seed, while chorizo is flavored with paprika and cumin.

Sauternes (*saw-terhn*)   *See* wine, sweet.

Sauvignon Blanc (*soh-vihn-yohn blahn*)   *See* wine, white.

savory   Savory comes in both a mild summer version and a more assertive winter version, but the flavor of this cousin of the mint family is like a cross between thyme and chervil. Substitute 50 percent thyme and 50 percent parsley.

savoy cabbage   *See* cabbage.

scallion   Also called green onions in some parts of the country, scallions are a member of the onion family with a flavor that's far milder than common onions. Spring onions, which are merely immature common onions, are slightly stronger in flavor than scallions but look similar. White and light green parts of leeks are another good substitution; however, they're slightly milder than scallions.

scallop   The tender texture and sweet flavor of this prized mollusk comes in two forms. Sea scallops, about 4 or 5 times the size of tiny bay scallops, have a slightly more savory and briny flavor. Sea scallops can be cut into quarters for recipes calling for bay scallops, but bay scallops should always be quickly sautéed or poached and should not be grilled. Alternatives for scallops are shrimp of the appropriate size (although they won't be as tender) or small pieces of monkfish.

Scotch bonnet chili   *See* chilies, fresh.

Scotch whiskey   *See* spirits.

scrod   *See* cod.

scup   *See* porgy.

sea bass   *See* black sea bass.

sea salt   *See* salt.

seatrout   *See* drum.

Seckel pear   *See* pear.

seitan (*SAY-tan*)   Due to its chewy texture, seitan is sometimes dubbed "wheat meat." It's made from wheat gluten and holds together well, which is why it's used in many vegetarian dishes. Firm tofu has the same bland flavor, and portobello mushroom caps are as chewy but add a woodsy flavor.

self-rising flour   *See* flour.

Sémillon (*say-mee-yohn*)   *See* wine, white.

semolina   Made from hard winter wheat, semolina is a coarsely milled flour; it's mostly used to make pasta dough, and almost all dried pasta is exclusively made from semolina. Semolina is available in most Italian markets. Bread flour, also high in hard wheat, is the best supermarket alternative.

serrano chili   *See* chilies, fresh.

Serrano ham   *See* ham.

sesame oil   *See* fats and oils.

sesame paste   *See* tahini.

sesame seed   Known as *benne seed* in Southern American cooking, sesame seeds come in both pearly white and jet black; there's no difference in the flavor. Finely chopped almonds create the same visual effect as white sesame seeds; sprinkle a few drops Asian sesame oil on them for flavor. Poppy seeds are the best alternative to black sesame seeds.

Seville orange   *See* orange.

sevruga (*sev-ROO-gah*)   *See* caviar.

shallot   This cousin of the onion has a mild flavor with garlic nuances, and it's formed more like a head of garlic with 2 or 3 large cloves per head covered with a thin, onionlike brown skin. To replicate the flavor, use finely chopped sweet onion, and add 1 minced garlic clove per ¼ cup chopped onion.

shark   Sharks are cartilaginous; they don't have a bony skeleton so there's a lot more delicious meat per fish. The pink flesh is firm and mild and turns white when cooked. Mako is the most popular shark for steaks or cubes, and dogfish, also called sand shark, has long been cooked for fish and chips in England. Swordfish, tuna, and mahi mahi are your best substitutes.

sherbet (*shur-bit*)   This frozen mixture, usually made from a fruit juice with the inclusion of a dairy product, is richer than sorbet but not as rich as ice cream. A light ice cream in the appropriate flavor is your best choice, or try a sorbet.

sherry   *See* wine, fortified.

shiitake (*she-tah-key*)   *See* mushroom, wild.

shiso (*she-soh*)   The leaves of this herb, also called perilla or Japanese basil, are either bright green or rusty red and jagged; both types have a refreshing and minty flavor. Lemon basil or mint can be used in its place.

short ribs   *See* beef.

short-grain rice   *See* rice.

shortening, vegetable   *See* fats and oils.

shoyu (*show-you*)   *See* soy sauce.

shrimp   These sweet-fleshed crustaceans are probably the most popular seafood in the country, from the classic cocktail to all sorts of sautéed and grilled dishes. Shrimp are classified by their size, which translates to the number per pound prior to peeling and *deveining*, called the *count*. Here are the major categories, from largest to the smallest:

Sub-Text

Deveining means to remove the black vein, actually the intestinal tract, from shrimp. Do this with the tip of a sharp paring knife or with a specialized tool called a deveiner. You should always devein large shrimp, but it's optional for small ones.

U-10s (or *colossal*)   These are huge because there's less than 10 to a pound. An alternative is rock lobster tails or monkfish fillets.

jumbo   There are 10 to 15 per pound in this category. Prawns are the best alternative—they even look like shrimp although they're a different species.

extra large   These are sometimes called "cocktail shrimp," and there are 16 to 20 per pound. Halved sea scallops can be cooked at the same rate.

large   By the time you get to the 21 to 30 per pound league, use bay scallops or small diced cubes of fish.

small   This count is 31 to 40 per pound. Use bay scallops or small diced cubes of fish.

tiny   Also called "salad shrimp," these always come prepeeled if not precooked. Crayfish tails are about the same size and flavor.

shrimp boil   *See* crab boil.

shrimp paste   Used in Asian cooking, this pungent and very fishy-tasting paste is made from fermented shrimp. Substitute anchovy paste in direct proportion.

simple syrup   This ingredient used in drinks is merely sugar and water that's been cooked so the sugar dissolves. The basic simple syrup is equal parts granulated sugar and water; bring it to a boil and simmer for 1 minute or until the liquid is clear.

sirloin   *See* beef.

skate   The large fins of this fish, called the wings, are the edible portions. They have a tender texture and sweet flavor. Sea scallops are your best alternative, and they cook in the same time.

skim milk   *See* milk.

skipjack   *See* tuna.

smelt   These small, shiny fish live in the sea but return to fresh water to spawn. They're about 3 inches long, and they're sold whole, either with or without the head. Best suited for pan-frying, herring and fresh anchovies are the best alternatives.

Smithfield ham   *See* ham.

smoked salmon   *See* salmon, smoked.

snails   The beloved escargot of France are one of the few univalves we eat, along with abalone and limpet, and they have a meaty texture. Littleneck clams and mussels are more tender, but they can be cooked in the same ways.

snow pea   Part of many Asian stir-fries, snow peas (after the tip is removed) are totally edible, which is why they're called *mange-tout* in French, or "eat it all." The only alternative is sugar snap peas; they're larger and require slightly longer cooking, but they, too, are totally edible.

Soave (*SUAVE-eh*)   *See* wine, white.

soba (*soh-buh*)   This Japanese noodle is made from buckwheat flour, which gives it a tan color and nutty flavor. Japanese ramen or any thin egg noodle can be substituted.

soft-shell clam   *See* clam.

soft-shell crab   *See* crab.

sole   This famed flatfish is best known for the species caught in European waters, the Dover sole. Some fish called sole in this country, such as lemon sole and Petrale sole, are technically members of the flounder family. Any flounder is the best substitution for sole, although turbot has a similar flavor.

soppressata (*soh-pres-SAH-tah*)   A specialty from the Treviso region of Italy, soppressata is closest to hard salami and pepperoni in both flavor and texture.

sorbet (*sore-bay*)   This French word for sherbet has taken on a different meaning; we now consider sorbet an ice with no dairy product while sherbet frequently includes milk. Any Italian ice, called *granita*, has the same formulation, although it's frequently coarser in texture.

sorrel   The sharp, acidic taste of the bright green leaves of this plant make it a favorite for soups and sauces. A 50-50 combination watercress and spinach replicates the flavor as well as the bright green color.

sour cream   Sour cream is sweet cream that's either had vinegar or a bacteria added to thicken it and create the tart flavor. Crème fraîche is the best substitute for sour cream, and as an added bonus, it can be brought to a boil in sauces without curdling. The flavor is not as sharp, however, so add 1 tablespoon lemon juice per 1 cup sour cream.

sour mash   *See* spirits.

soy milk   Soy milk, made by boiling ground soybeans, looks like cow's milk but it has more protein and iron and less fat. Cow's milk or rice milk can be used in its place.

soy sauce   You can find hundreds of formulations of this Asian seasoning, all of which start from a base of fermented soybeans. Most can be used interchangeably, except for Chinese black soy, which has molasses added. Other alternatives are tamari, which is slightly sweeter, and fish sauce (*nam pla*), which is salty but also adds a pungent fish flavor.

soybean   *See* edamame.

soybean curd   *See* tofu.

soybean oil   *See* fats and oils.

spaghetti   *See* pasta, dried.

spaghetti squash   A member of the winter squash family, the cooked flesh of this football-shape squash comes out in thin, light green strands resembling spaghetti when you comb it with the tines of a fork. No vegetables cook the same way, so the only alternative for the strands is to use a thin pasta such as angel hair. Zucchini and yellow squash have the same mild flavor.

Spanish onion   *See* onion.

spareribs   *See* pork.

spaetzle (*SHPEHT-sehl*)   These egg noodles popular in Germany and Austria are hand formed so they're irregular in shape. The basic formulation is egg noodle dough, so a medium egg noodle can take its place.

spearmint   *See* mint.

spinach   With its slightly bitter flavor, spinach is one of the most versatile vegetables. It can be enjoyed raw, or it cooks in a matter of seconds. If eating it raw, substitute escarole or frisée for the flavor. If eating it cooked, broccoli rabe or Swiss chard are the best options, although they both take longer to cook.

spiny lobster   *See* rock lobster.

spirits   Sprits are distilled beverages that contain at least 35 percent ethyl alcohol purified by distillation from a fermented substance that can be various grains, vegetables, or fruits. What distinguishes spirits from liqueurs that are of equal alcohol content is that spirits are low in sugar.

Here are the various types commonly found in drink and food recipes:

blended whisky   This generic whisky varies from brand to brand and comes from the fermentation of different cereal grains. Bourbon or Scotch are the best substitutes.

Bourbon   A whisky must be distilled in the state of Kentucky to be called Bourbon, and it has to be made primarily from corn. Sour mash is similar in flavor although milder, but it's the best for drinking. Bourbon is also used frequently in sauces, both for savory dishes and desserts. In those circumstances, either rum or brandy can be used.

Canadian whisky   Crown Royal and Canadian Club are the two most popular brands of Canadian whisky. Generic blended whisky, rye, or Irish whiskey can be substituted.

gin   The dominant flavor of gin is that of the juniper berries fermented in the grains along with herbs and spices. Vodka is the closest spirit to substitute; however, it doesn't have the juniper flavor. Aquavit, a Scandinavian liqueur flavored with caraway, is another option.

S

Irish whiskey   There's a peat flavor to Irish whiskey that's similar to Scotch, which is the best substitute. Other options are Canadian whisky or blended whisky.

mescal   Like tequila, mescal is made from the agave plant, but in this case, it's fire-roasted before the sap is extracted to distill. Tequila is the best alternative, although it lacks the smoky undertaste.

rum   This famous spirit made from the distillation of sugar cane runs the gamut from clear and white to almost black; the darker ones have a flavor of molasses. Any rum can be substituted for another, and a fruit brandy such as kirsch is another option. For a nonalcoholic option, substitute 1 teaspoon rum extract stirred into ½ cup water or apple juice for each ½ cup rum.

rye   Rye is named for the primary grain from which it's distilled, and it's similar in style to Bourbon but not quite as smooth. Bourbon or sour mash are the best alternatives.

Scotch   There's a very distinctive smoky flavor to Scotch, and two categories of beverages can be classified as Scotch. The most refined are the single-malt distillations that have a more complex flavor than their blended relatives. Irish whiskey, although it lacks the smoky nuances, is the best substitute.

sour mash   Sometimes called Tennessee whiskey, this brew tastes a lot like Bourbon but the mash is allowed to sour during the fermenting process. Jack Daniels is the best-known brand. Bourbon is the best alternative, although it's not as dry.

tequila   This fiery brew is predominantly made in Mexico from fermented blue agave cactus sap. It comes both clear and in an amber shade. Mescal or vodka are the best substitutions; white rum is another alternative.

vodka   Basic vodka is a colorless and almost flavorless distillation of ethanol purified with grains or potato skins. It's difficult to substitute because all other spirits have a distinct flavor profile. Tequila is about the best, or you can substitute 50 percent ethyl alcohol and 50 percent water.

split pea   *See* beans, dried.

sprout *See* bean sprout.

spumante (*spoo-MAHN-tay*)   *See* wine, sparkling.

squab *See* game bird.

squid   Frequently sold by its Italian name, *calamari*, this cephalopod is gaining popularity around the world for its mild flavor that responds best to either very quick cooking like frying or sautéing or slow braising. Baby octopus is not as tender, but for braising, it has a similar flavor but requires a longer cooking time. For frying, cuttlefish is an alternative, although it's harder to find than squid.

star anise   This spice used primarily in Chinese cooking looks like a flower with eight petals and has more aroma than Western anise seed.

> *1 whole star anise = $\frac{1}{2}$ tsp. anise seed + pinch allspice, $\frac{1}{2}$ tsp. Chinese five-spice powder, or 2 tsp. anise liqueur such as Pernod*

star fruit (or **carambola**)   When you cut this fruit into thin slices, it actually looks like stars. The flavor of the ripe fruit is a combination of lemon, plum, and pineapple, and thin slices of pineapple have the same golden color. Unripe star fruit is very astringent and can be used as a garnish for beverages; lemon slices are the best alternative.

stewing chicken *See* chicken.

sticky rice *See* rice.

Stilton *See* cheese.

stock   Made by slowly simmering vegetables and frequently some sort of protein in water, stocks form the backbone of most great soups and sauces. If you don't have any homemade, look for a canned or packaged stock that's either organic or low-salt. Or mix 1 cup boiling water with 1 teaspoon bouillon powder of the appropriate flavor. You can also use 1 package gravy mix for each 1 cup stock in the appropriate flavor; it adds a thickening agent, but the flavor is similar.

stout *See* beer.

strawberry   For the same bright red color, raspberries are the only choice among the berries, although diced plums give fruit salads a similar color.

string bean *See* green bean.

striped bass (or **striper**)   The flesh of this saltwater fish is firm and the flavor is sweet. Red snapper and grouper have the same taste and texture.

sturgeon   Overfishing almost decimated the sturgeon population in the nineteenth century. In addition to being the source of fine caviar, the flesh of sturgeon has a firm texture and mild flavor. Pike is the best substitution for both these qualities.

suet   This hard fat is found around the kidneys of cows and sheep. It's traditionally been used as the fat in English steamed plum pudding and in the mincemeat filling for pies. Butter or lard are good substitutions, as is vegetable shortening for a vegetarian option.

sugar   In addition to providing sweetness, sugar tenderizes baked goods. Each of the leading options for sugars has its own unique qualities and flavor characteristics:

confectioners' (or *powdered*)   This powdered, granulated sugar has 3 to 4 percent cornstarch added to improve stability and to prevent caking. Do not substitute it for granulated sugar, or visa versa, especially in liquids (confectioners' will make them cloudy). Confectioners' sugar works well in whipped cream because the cornstarch keeps the mixture from separating. To make your own confectioners' sugar, blend ¾ cup granulated sugar and 1 teaspoon cornstarch in a blender for each 1 cup confectioners' sugar.

dark brown or *light brown*   This is granulated sugar that has been flavored with molasses. Dark brown sugar has a deeper color and more intense flavor than light brown sugar, but the two can be used interchangeably. To make brown sugar from granulated sugar, add 2 tablespoons molasses per 1 cup sugar for light brown or 3 tablespoons for dark brown. To make light brown sugar into dark brown, add 1 tablespoon molasses per cup. If adding molasses, reduce the liquid in a recipe by the amount added.

granulated   Granulated sugar caramelizes and turns brown when heated, giving foods their characteristic aroma and color. This is the most common sugar, and when a recipe calls for sugar, granulated sugar is implied.

superfine   This is granulated sugar that's been more finely milled. Granulated sugar can be substituted on a one-for-one basis. If texture is important to a finished product, you can pulverize granulated sugar in a blender. Superfine sugar results in a finer crumb and lighter texture in baked goods.

sugar snap pea   As with snow peas, sugar snaps are entirely edible, although the peas inside the pod are larger than those of snow peas. Snow peas are the best substitute; cook them for half the time of sugar snaps. Or you can use julienne green beans cut to the same length as a sugar snap.

sugar syrup   *See* simple syrup.

sultana   *See* raisin.

summer savory   *See* savory.

sunchoke   *See* Jerusalem artichoke.

sun-dried tomato   *See* tomato, sun-dried.

sunflower oil   *See* fats and oils.

sunflower seed   Unlike pumpkin and squash seeds, the seeds of this huge flower, so named because it turns its "face" to the sun all day, must be shelled before eating them. Most of the time you can find them preshelled and preroasted. Pumpkin seeds and large acorn or butternut squash seeds are the best substitutions.

sushi rice   *See* rice.

sweet basil   *See* basil.

sweet marjoram   *See* marjoram.

sweet potato   *See* yam.

sweet woodruff   *See* woodruff.

sweetbreads   With a satiny, delicate texture and flavor, sweetbreads—actually the thymus gland of a calf—are a delicacy; the name is always plural because they come in pairs. Veal brains have the same texture as sweetbreads, although veal scallops have a closer flavor.

sweetened condensed milk   *See* milk, sweetened condensed.

Swiss chard   *See* greens.

Swiss cheese   *See* cheese.

swordfish   Mild-tasting swordfish, always cut into steaks rather than fillets, has very firm and fine-grained flesh. The smooth black skin helps hold the flesh together while the swordfish is cooking, but should not be eaten. Shark and halibut come closest to swordfish in flavor and color; tuna is another option, but the flesh is darker.

Syrah (*see-RAWH*)   *See* wine, red.

Szechwan peppercorn   *See* peppercorn.

Tabasco sauce   *See* hot red pepper sauce.

tahini (*tah-HEE-knee*)   This paste made from ground sesame seeds is crucial to the success of dishes like hummus. Make it yourself by grinding white sesame seeds in a blender with enough sesame oil to make it into a smooth paste. Or use unsweetened almond butter; both peanut butter and cashew butter add too much of their distinct flavor.

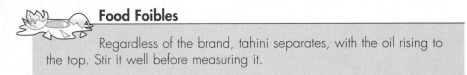

Food Foibles

Regardless of the brand, tahini separates, with the oil rising to the top. Stir it well before measuring it.

Taleggio (*tal-LEH-j'yoh*)   *See* cheese.

tamari (*tah-mar-e*)   Made from fermented soy beans, tamari is used primarily as a condiment or dipping sauce for Asian dishes. It's thicker and has a more complex flavor than soy sauce, but soy sauce remains the best alternative.

tamarillo (*tah-mar-REE-yoh*)   This South American fruit is egg-shaped and grows in both yellow and red. Its blushing pink flesh is usually squeezed for drinks. Papaya and mango are the best substitutions both for color and flavor.

tamarind (*TAH-mar-ind*)   The pulp from the tamarind pods are used as a sour accent in Latin American, Indian, and many Middle Eastern cuisines. Equal amounts of lemon or lime juice can be substituted.

tangelo   A cross between a tangerine and a pomelo, tangelos can range from clementine size to small grapefruit size. Any member of the mandarin orange family or a common navel orange can be used as an alternative.

tangerine   *See* mandarin orange.

tapioca   Made from the roots of a cassava plant, tapioca comes in many forms. The large granules, called pearl tapioca, are used to make the creamy pudding, and either instant tapioca or tapioca flour are used as a thickening agent, especially for fruit pies. For pearl tapioca, substitute short-grain rice in recipes. To thicken with tapioca:

> *1 TB. instant tapioca = 2 TB. cornstarch mixed with 2 TB. cold water, or 3 TB. all-purpose flour*

taro root   Any visitor to Hawaii has probably sampled taro root; it's the basis for poi. It's a tuber, and the slightly sweet flesh has a somewhat purplish cast. Purple potatoes can be substituted; add a bit of sugar or coconut pulp to add a touch of sweetness.

tarragon   The slender, pointed green leaves of this member of the aster family has a mild anise or licorice flavor.

> *1 TB. chopped fresh tarragon = 1 tsp. dried tarragon, ³⁄₄ tsp. crushed anise seeds, or 2 tsp. anise liqueur such as Pernod*

tartar sauce   This mayonnaise-based sauce is used most often as a dipping sauce for fried fish, but it's also delicious for any poultry dish.

T

Yield: 2 cups

1½ cups mayonnaise
3 TB. chopped scallion
2 TB. finely chopped dill
  pickle
2 TB. sweet pickle relish

2 TB. freshly squeezed lemon
  juice
1 TB. small capers
2 TB. Dijon mustard
Salt and hot red pepper

Stir together mayonnaise, scallion, dill pickle, relish, lemon juice, capers, and Dijon mustard, and season with salt and hot red pepper sauce. Store refrigerated for up to 4 days, tightly covered.

tasso (*tass-oh*)   *See* ham.

tempeh (*TEM-peh*)   This vegetarian meat replacement is made from fermented cooked soybeans and has a chewy texture, nutty flavor, and a consistency similar to firm tofu. Either tofu or seitan are good substitutions.

temple orange   *See* oranges.

tenderloin   *See* beef; pork.

tepín   *See* chilies, dried.

tequila (*teh-KEY-lah*)   *See* spirits.

terrine   *See* pâté.

Thai ginger   *See* galangal.

Thai pepper.   *See* chilies, fresh.

Thousand Island dressing   *See* Russian dressing.

thyme   This member of the mint family has tiny, gray-green leaves and a flavor that's a cross between mint and tea. Both herbes de Provence and Italian seasoning contain thyme, along with other herbs, so its flavor will be included.

  1 TB. fresh thyme = 1 tsp. dried

Tía Maria   *See* liqueur.

tilapia (*tih-LAH-pee-uh*)   This native African fish is now widely aqua-cultured around the world, and its low-fat flesh is sweet and fine-textured. Sole, flounder, and porgy are the best substitutes for these thin fillets.

tilefish   A diet of crab gives the flesh of tilefish its incredibly delicate flavor. Also called ocean whitefish, the fillets are usually rather thick, so sea bass or mahi mahi are your best choices.

Tillamook cheese   *See* cheese.

tobiko (*toe-bee-koh*)   *See* caviar.

toffee   Like caramel, toffee is made by cooking sugar and water until it's colored brown, at which time some cream or butter is frequently added. Caramels are almost identical in texture and flavor.

tofu   Tofu is a custardlike substance, also called bean curd (the literal translation from Chinese). Tofu's texture depends on the amount of water that's been pressed out. You will find three different consistencies in the supermarket:

> *soft* (or *silken*)   This tofu has had no water removed and has the texture of silky custard. It's great added to smoothies or juices, but it doesn't hold together when cooked. Soy yogurt is the best substitute.

> *firm*   Some whey has been pressed out, so this tofu has the texture of raw meat, although that texture won't change when it's cooked. It bounces back when pressed with your finger and can easily be picked up by chopsticks or a fork. Tempeh has more flavor, but it's still a soy-based product; seitan, made from wheat gluten, is another alternative.

> *dry*   The most solid of all tofu, it has the texture of cooked meat and crumbles easily. This type of tofu is used in processed tofu products. If you're not concerned about using a dairy product, Indian paneer cheese is a good choice, or you can use tempeh or seitan.

Tokaji Aszú (*toe-ki as-zuh*)   *See* wine, dessert.

tomatillo (*toe-mah-TEA-yoh*)   These hard, apple-green balls covered in a paperlike husk resemble tomatoes, although they're not related botanically. Used extensively in Mexican cooking, tomatillos have a tart flavor with a slight citrus note. Unripe green tomatoes are an excellent substitute; add a few drops of lime juice to replicate the citrus note.

tomato   To me, fresh vine-ripened tomatoes are one of the glories of summer, and now that many growers are reviving heirloom species, there's even variety in the color beyond the ubiquitous red and the occasional orange and yellow. Any tomato can be substituted for each other, and it's preferable to use canned tomatoes in cooking rather than immature fresh tomatoes. One large tomato equals 1 cup, chopped, so if using smaller tomatoes in place of a large one, use that measure as the guide.

1 lb. fresh tomatoes = 1½ cups canned tomatoes, drained or 4 TB. tomato paste

tomato, sun-dried   Most tomatoes are oven-dried rather than sun-dried, but they come both loose and packed in olive oil. The dehydration gives these tomatoes a sweet and intense tomato flavor.

4 sun-dried tomato halves = 1 TB. sun-dried tomato paste or 2 TB. tomato paste

tomato juice   Use equal parts tomato sauce and water to replicate the flavor and consistency.

tomato paste   This thick paste comes from simmering tomatoes for many hours to evaporate the liquid and then straining it to achieve a smooth texture. Tomato paste delivers a very intense flavor without adding liquid to dishes.

1 TB. tomato paste = 2 sun-dried tomato halves, puréed or 4 TB. tomato sauce (reduce other liquid in recipe, or boil down sauce to 1 TB.)

tomato sauce   Most brands of tomato sauce have some seasoning added, so when substituting, you'll have to compensate with some salt.

1 cup tomato sauce = ⅓ cup tomato paste + ⅔ cup water, or 1½ cups canned diced tomatoes, drained and puréed

tongue   An organ meat, tongue comes from cows, calves, and sheep. It must always be braised or boiled and peeled before eating. For sandwiches, corned beef and pastrami are good alternatives. For braising and saucing, use any cut from the same animal appropriate for braising.

tortellini (*tohr-teh-LEE-nee*)   *See* pasta, stuffed.

tortilla, corn (*tore-TEE-yah*)   This mainstay of the Mexican diet is made from a cornmeal paste and cooked on a griddle. If you can't find corn tortillas, use flour ones.

tortilla, flour   A corn flatbread is difficult to find in cuisines other than Mexican, but flour-based flatbreads are popular around the world. Pita bread cut in half, soft lavash, or naan are all good substitutes for flour tortillas.

tree ear (or **tree fungus**)   *See* mushroom, Asian dried.

Triple Sec   *See* liqueur.

trout   The rainbow trout, a colorful freshwater fish, is probably the best known of this family of fatty, flaky-textured fish. Most are sold whole because their weight is about 10 ounces boned. Whitefish, salmon, and perch are the best substitutions for a similar delicate flavor and high oil content.

trout, smoked   Pale trout fillets become a delicate smoked fish. Smoked whitefish is the best substitution.

truffle   *See* mushroom, wild.

tuna   Numbers of tuna species are found in waters all over the world, from 5-pound bonita to 1,500-pound bluefin. All have firm, fine-grained pinkish-red to dark-red flesh that's hearty and chewy. Tuna began to gain popularity in this country served raw as sushi, and most people prefer cooked tuna to remain rare when cooked; it's sometimes called the "aquatic filet mignon." The most common species of tuna are ahi, aku, blackfin, bluefin, bonita, skipjack, and yellowfin, and all can be substituted for one another successfully. Swordfish and shark are the two best alternatives for tuna for the texture, and if you want a fish with color, choose salmon.

turban squash   This winter squash got its name because the round shape with a protrusion coming from the top makes it look like a turban. Acorn or butternut squash or pumpkin can all be used in its place.

turbot   Native to the waters off northern Europe, this flatfish has a mild flavor and firm, lean flesh. Sole and flounder have similar attributes, and halibut is another option.

turkey   Long gone are the days that turkey is reserved for presentation on Thanksgiving and/or Christmas. The popularity of this flavorful bird has grown in tandem with chicken. For white meat, turkey and chicken can be used interchangeably; veal scallops or pork tenderloin have a slightly richer flavor that can work, too. For dark meat turkey, try goose or duck in addition to dark meat chicken; they'll be slightly richer than turkey and have nuances of a gamey flavor.

> Few people can pass up a piece of golden, crispy turkey skin, but that's where almost half the saturated fat calories are housed. Cook a turkey with the skin on to keep it moist, but then throw out the skin before serving.

turkey, ground   Ground turkey has a richer flavor than ground chicken, but the latter works as an alternative. Ground veal and ground pork can be substituted, too, and have the same light color once cooked.

turmeric   This root of a tropical plant is botanically related to ginger; it has a bitter flavor but is most known for the bright yellow-orange color it gives food. Saffron, although far more expensive, gives food the same color. Curry powder adds a number of other spices and flavors into a dish, but turmeric is a primary ingredient.

turnip   Turnips look like root vegetables, but they're actually a member of the cabbage family, which accounts for their somewhat assertive flavor. They come in white, purple, and combinations of both, but the flesh is white and crisp when raw. For a purée, a 50-50 combination of rutabaga and parsnip produces almost the same flavor because rutabagas are more bitter and parsnips are sweeter.

turnip greens   *See* greens.

turtle bean   *See* beans, dried.

udon (*oo-dohn*)   These Japanese noodles are wheat-based and look very much like spaghetti. Substitute spaghetti cut into 3-inch lengths.

ugli fruit (*ugly*)   The ugli fruit is an exercise in genetic engineering; it's a cross between a grapefruit and a tangerine. The flesh under the thick skin is more tart than sweet, so a ruby red grapefruit is your best alternative.

Toque Tips

Pomelos, actually raised for their thick rind, are very difficult to find, so if you want to make a candied citrus peel, use an ugli fruit.

unsalted butter   *See* butter.

unsweetened cocoa powder   *See* chocolate.

V

vacherin (*vash-rahn*)   *See* cheese.

Valencia orange   *See* orange.

Valpolicella (*vahl-poh-lee-CHEH-lah*)   *See* wine, red.

vanilla extract   Few recipes for sweetened baked goods don't call for at least a few drops of vanilla extract. You can substitute another extract such as almond, brandy, or rum in the same amount. You can also use a vanilla bean; 1 inch vanilla bean equals 1 teaspoon vanilla extract. Scrape the seeds out of the pod, and add the seeds and pod to the liquid to be added to the recipe. Allow the mixture to simmer for 5 minutes and then let it cool. Or you can use a flavored liquor or liqueur such as rum, kirsch, amaretto, triple sec, or brandy in the ratio of 1 tablespoon liquor per 1 teaspoon vanilla. Adjust the other liquids in the recipe accordingly.

Toque Tips

Pure vanilla extract is much more expensive than the imitation, but it makes such a difference in the flavor and aroma of a dish, even when used in minute quantities. Always splurge and buy the real thing.

veal   Pork producers have built a campaign about pork being "the other white meat," but veal is even more delicate and is a luxurious meat regardless of whether it's braised, sautéed, or roasted. Veal comes from calves up to 6 months old that weigh no more than 200 to 250 pounds.

Despite its tenderness, veal is not ideal for cooking over high heat, as it has little natural fat. Roasting and broiling must be done with care, and by using lower heat than for other meats.

Pork, chicken, and turkey are natural alternatives to veal; cook each to the appropriate interior temperature. If you're wondering how to substitute one cut of veal for another, refer to the following table.

Veal at a Glance

Veal	Description	Cooking Methods
Arm steaks	tender	sauté, fry
Blade steaks	tender	sauté, fry
Boned shoulder	less tender	braise, stew
Breast	least tender, fatty	braise
Center leg	very tender	slow roast
Crown roast	very tender	slow roast
Cutlet	tender	sauté
Loin chops	very tender	grill, sauté
Loin roast	very tender	slow roast
Saddle	very tender	roast
Shank (osso buco)	less tender	braise

When cooking veal or any meat, you need to know how much to cook per person, especially if you're substituting a cut with bones for one without. The following table helps you determine how much you'll need.

Veal per Person

Cut	With Bone	Without Bone
Boned shoulder	n/a	10 oz.
Breast	1 lb.	10 oz.

continues

Veal per Person   (continued)

Cut	With Bone	Without Bone
Cutlets	n/a	4 to 6 oz.
Loin chop	12 oz.	8 oz.
Loin roast	12 oz.	8 oz.
Shanks	1 (16 oz.)	n/a

veal, ground   As is the case with parts of veal, ground turkey, chicken, and pork are the best substitutions.

vegetable oil   *See* fats and oils.

vegetable oil spray   Vegetable oil spray is rarely if ever used as an ingredient; it's used as a way to coat surfaces with very little fat in a simple way, be it a casserole or baking sheet to prevent sticking, or to create a crispy crust on a food rather than frying it in a large quantity of oil. For the former use, moisten a paper towel with oil and rub it on the surface. To use as a crisping agent, blot the food with a paper towel soaked in oil.

vegetable shortening   *See* fats and oils.

velouté sauce   *See* white sauce.

venison   *See* game meat.

Vermentino (*vehr-mehn-TEE-noh*)   *See* wine, red.

vermicelli (*vehr-mee-CHEH-lee*)   *See* pasta, dried.

vermouth   *See* wine, fortified.

vialone nano (*vee-ah-LONE-eh NAH-noh*)   *See* rice.

Vidalia onion   *See* onion.

vin santo (*veen SAHN-toh*)   *See* wine, dessert.

vinaigrette   Vinaigrette dressings are not only the most frequent way to dress tossed salads, the dressings are increasingly used as sauces to season grilled foods as well.

The generally accepted ratio is approximately 3 parts oil to 1 part vinegar, lemon juice, or lime juice. This ratio can vary depending on the vinegar's acid level. To cut back on the fat in a dressing, use a mild citrus juice such as orange or grapefruit juice along with a stronger acid; or add chicken stock.

Any bottled salad dressing can be used in place of a vinaigrette, or the acid can be the liquid in which pickles are stored.

Toque Tips

The proper amount of dressing is 1½ to 2 tablespoons for a side salad. Begin by using only ⅔ of the dressing you think you'll need. Lettuces should be dressed lightly, not doused.

vinegar   All vinegars have acetic acid, no matter what basic ingredient is used to produce the actual vinegar. Various wines, malt, cider, and rice are the most commonly used vinegars, and each has its own unique flavor.

Freshly squeezed lemon or lime juice can be used in place of vinegar, especially wine vinegars because they have the same tart acidity. If you want to substitute one vinegar for another, here's an overview of vinegars commonly listed in recipes:

balsamic   Native to Italy and tremendously popular due to its mild, almost sweet flavor, balsamic vinegar is made from unfermented grape juice that has aged for 10 years. Rice vinegar is equally mild.

cider   Made from apple juice and processed much the same way as wine vinegar, cider vinegar has a strong, sharp taste and a light brown color. Malt vinegar is the best substitution.

malt   A strong vinegar most often used for pickling vegetables, malt vinegar is made from barley malt. It can be clear, light brown, or dark brown if caramel is added. Cider vinegar is an alternative with a similar taste.

rice (or *rice wine vinegar*)   The mildest of the vinegars, rice vinegar is made from fermented rice wine. It's especially popular in Japanese and Chinese dishes, and it comes both colorless and light brown.

V

white distilled This is your basic vinegar; it's distilled from ethyl alcohol and lacks the subtlety of most other vinegars. Cider vinegar is the best substitution.

wine The intensity of the wine determines the flavor of the vinegar. Red and white wine vinegars are more assertive than champagne vinegar or sherry vinegar. All the wines are fermented under controlled conditions until the sugar is converted to acetic acid. It's then filtered—water is added, pasteurized, and bottled. Cider vinegar is most often used as a substitute for all wine vinegars.

vinho verde (*VEE-no VEHR-day*) *See* wine, white.

Viognier (*veen-yon-ay*) *See* wine, white.

Virginia ham *See* ham.

vodka *See* spirits.

Vouvray (*voo-vray*) *See* wine, white.

wahoo This warm-water fish, called *ono* if caught in Hawaiian waters, is related to the king mackerel, which is the best substitute because it has the same sweet flesh that's moderately high in fat. Mahi mahi and swordfish also work.

Walla Walla onion *See* onion.

walleyed pike *See* perch.

walnut   What we find most often are English walnuts; the other variety is black walnuts that have a more assertive flavor but it takes a sledge hammer to remove the shell. Pecans and hazelnuts are the best substitutions because they have the same moderate flavor.

walnut oil   *See* oil, nut.

wasabi (*wah-sah-bee*)   This potent and pungent Japanese horseradish is sold in both powdered and paste forms; it's mixed with soy sauce as a dipping sauce for sushi and sashimi. Substitute prepared Western horseradish at the ratio of 2 teaspoons horseradish per 1 teaspoon wasabi.

water chestnut   You can occasionally find freshwater chestnuts in Asian markets, but the canned form of these crisp additions to Chinese dishes are far more common. Fresh jicama has a similar crunchy texture and sweet flavor.

watercress   *See* lettuce.

watermelon   This is one of those unique foods for which finding a substitution isn't easy. No other melon has the same blushing pink color or the same level of water. Honeydew melon, while pale green, has a similar sweet flavor.

wax bean   *See* green bean.

weakfish   *See* drum.

weisswurst (*VICE-voorst*)   This mild-flavored white sausage is traditionally served in Germany in the fall. White bratwurst or French boudin blanc are the best substitutions.

Westphalian ham   *See* ham.

wheat berries   These whole kernels of wheat just have the inedible hull removed. Cracked wheat and bulgur are first cousins and cook in less time.

W

Toque Tips

Like dried beans, wheat berries are extremely hard. Presoaking for a few hours in cold water makes them cook much faster.

wheat bran   This fiber-rich covering of wheat berries doesn't have much flavor, but it does boost the fiber in any number of dishes. Oat bran or wheat germ are the best substitutions.

wheat germ   You'll find lots of vitamins and minerals in this nutritious embryo found inside the kernel. Wheat germ is almost always sold toasted and should be kept refrigerated after it's opened. Wheat bran or oat bran deliver the same bulk in a recipe.

whipping cream   *See* cream.

whiskey   *See* spirits.

white beans   *See* beans, dried.

white chocolate   *See* chocolate.

white pepper   *See* peppercorn.

white sauce   From creamed soups to the binding for croquettes, white sauces are a backbone of all European cuisines. What we call white sauce is actually two families of French sauces; béchamel sauces are made with milk or cream and velouté sauces are made with stock. Both families start with a flour and fat roux.

Yield: 2 cups

2 TB. unsalted butter
3 TB. all-purpose flour
2 cups milk or stock

Salt and freshly ground white pepper

Melt butter in a saucepan over low heat. Add flour, and cook over low heat, stirring constantly, for 2 minutes. Slowly add milk and whisk well. Bring to a boil, whisking frequently, and simmer 2 minutes. Season with salt and pepper.

---

white vinegar   *See* vinegar.

whitefish   These freshwater fish are found in deep, cold lakes and streams in Canada and the states that border it. Whitefish are generally about 7 pounds, and smaller ones are called chubs. Pike and sturgeon are the best alternatives.

whitefish, smoked The high fat content of whitefish means that even once smoked, the flesh is very moist. Smoked sturgeon has the same white color and a very similar flavor.

whiting *See* cod.

whole-wheat flour *See* flour.

wild boar *See* game meat.

wild rice Wild rice is a very distant cousin of Asian rice; North America's only native species is really an aquatic grass, *Zizania aquatica*. It has a nutty flavor similar to brown rice, wheat berries, and kasha, so use one of those in its place.

wine, apéritif These wines are served before dinner to stimulate the appetite; true aficionados believe they do so without dulling the taste buds, as may happen with a drink made with spirits.

Apéritif Wines at a Glance

Wine	Origin	Substitution
Campari	Italy	This bitter bright red drink is frequently mixed with either soda water or tonic, but many people also sip it straight either on the rocks or neat. Sweet vermouth with a few shots of bitters is about the only combination that replicates the flavor, which is a guarded secret.
Dubonnet	France	White Dubonnet has the same herbal flavor as dry vermouth, so either it or a dry sherry can be substituted. For Dubonnet red, sweet vermouth is a good alternative, as is a very sweet sherry. Both versions of this wine apéritif are also made by Lillet and can be substituted equally.

continues

W

Apéritif Wines at a Glance (continued)

Wine	Origin	Substitution
Lillet	France	Lillet, made in the wine-rich region of Bordeaux, has the same dry and sweet versions as Dubonnet, but it has more complexity to the flavor. Dubonnet can be substituted, or use the substitutions listed for Dubonnet.

wine, dessert   For many people—including me—a glass of dessert wine can be dessert itself. These sweet wines, all of which are served chilled, are made in a variety of ways. Some wines are enriched with honey or sugar, but most are formed by a fungus referred to as "noble rot." This mold, *Botrytis cinerea*, sucks water out of the grapes, concentrating their sugar.

Ice wines are another large category of dessert wines. For these wines, the grapes are allowed to remain on the vine and shrivel until they freeze. This method also concentrates the sugars. Wines termed "late harvest" are always dessert wines because the grapes are allowed to ripen on the vines almost until they become raisins.

Both Port and Madeira are fortified wines served as dessert wines, but a host of wines from many countries meet the requirement of being even sweeter than the food with which they're served. Any of the dessert wines can be substituted for each other.

Dessert Wines at a Glance

Wine	Origin	Characteristics
Banyuls	France	red wine, good with chocolate
Barsac	France	lighter than Sauternes
Beerenauslese	Austria	very rich and syrupy
Eiswein	Various	light and fruity
Moscato	Italy	very fruity

Wine	Origin	Characteristics
Muscat	France	frequently fortified
Reisling, late harvest	Various	lighter than Sauternes
Sauternes	France	notes of honey and caramel
Tokaji Aszú	Hungary	similar to Sauternes
Vin Santo	Italy	generic sweet wine, served with biscotti
Zinfandel, late harvest	USA	a good alternative to Banyuls

wine, fortified   These wines have been fortified with some other type of alcohol and frequently have been flavored with herbs or spices, or have had additional sugar added. They're frequently used in cooking, especially sherry and marsala. When they're served alone, it's most often as an apéritif at the beginning of a meal or along with dessert. For an apéritif, you can always substitute a sparkling wine or a mixed drink. As a dessert wine, look for choices in that entry.

Fortified Wines at a Glance

Wine	Origin*	Substitution
Madeira	Portugal	Like sherry, Madeira runs the gamut from very dry to very sweet. The driest is Sercial Madeira, for which marsala or a dry Port is a good substitute. For a Bual Madeira, any sweet dessert wine or Port can be served.
marsala	Italy	This Italian wine is the dominant ingredient in such classic dishes as veal marsala or zabaglione. Use Madeira or equal parts sherry and sweet vermouth as an alternative.

W

continues

Fortified Wines at a Glance   (continued)

Wine	Origin*	Substitution
Port	Portugal	Named for the port city of Porto at the mouth of the Douro River, Port is fortified with distilled grape spirits. A well-aged Madeira is the best alternative.
sherry	Spain	Sherry is fortified with brandy and all are naturally dry; if sweet, sugar has been added at a later time. Madeira or a dry Port are the best substitutions for a dry sherry. Japanese mirin, a rice wine, is slightly sweet. For a sweet "cream" sherry, substitute sweet vermouth.
vermouth (dry)	Italy/ France	This vermouth is used to make martinis and as a cooking ingredient. For a martini, use sake or turn the drink into a gimlet by adding Rose's lime juice. As an ingredient, use any dry white wine or dry sherry.
vermouth (sweet)	Italy/ France	This vermouth is used in such cocktails as Manhattans and Negronis, and it comes both as a blushing red and in a white version. Sweet Madeira or an apéritif such as Dubonnet make good substitutions.

Although many lesser-quality fortified wines are produced around the world, the country listed here is where the wine originated.

wine, red   It's very confusing to differentiate both red and white table wines, also called still wines, from sparkling wine, because wines are marketed both by the name of the predominant grape and by the location of its production. For example, a wine labeled Pinot Noir is produced from grapes of that varietal and can come from the United States, New Zealand, or Chile. However, most of the famed red wines of the Burgundy region of France are made entirely from Pinot Noir but are labeled Burgundy.

For cooking, you can substitute almost any red wine for any other. But drinking is another matter. The best way to determine what wine to substitute for what wine is by the flavor characteristics of that wine. This can change from producer to producer and vintage to vintage, but your best choice is to use the same body of the wine.

Red Wines at a Glance

Wine	Characteristics
Barbaresco	powerful
Barbera	earthy, rich
Bardolino	rich, fruity
Barolo	powerful
Beaujolais	juicy, fruity
Brunello di Montalcino	soft, earthy
Cabernet Sauvignon	rich, powerful
Châteauneuf-du-Pape	delicate, earthy
Chianti	earthy
Dolcetto	fruity, delicate
Grenache	fruity, delicate
Malbec	rich, earthy
Merlot	rich, soft
Nebbiolo	powerful
Petite Syrah	rich, earthy

W

continues

Red Wines at a Glance   (contiunued)

Wine	Characteristics
Pinot Noir	delicate, earthy
Rioja	earthy
Sangiovese	earthy
Syrah	powerful, rich
Valpolicella	earthy
Zinfandel	fruity, rich

wine, sparkling   Although we use the term *champagne* generically, only sparkling wine from that French region is truly champagne; the others go by various names or just the descriptive term *sparkling wine*. The wine is "sparkling" because it contains carbon dioxide, the same gas that gives carbonated sodas their fizz.

Spumante is the generic term for Italian sparkling wine, and Asti Spumante is its chief producer. The other Italian sparkling wine of note is prosecco. Any sparkling wine can be substituted for another, and nonalcoholic sparkling wines are available as alternatives as well. Sauvignon Blanc, Chablis, and white Bordeaux are the best substitutes for sparkling wines.

wine, white   For cooking, almost any white wine can be substituted for any other, and it's not necessary to spend a lot of money on a wine for cooking. You can substitute dry vermouth in small quantities for white wine, but not in large quantities because the herbal character of the vermouth can dominate a dish. Nonalcoholic white wines are available and are a good option for cooking. In a pinch, you can also substitute chicken stock for poultry dishes and seafood stock for fish dishes.

The best way to determine what drinking wine to substitute is by the flavor characteristics. While this can change from producer to producer and vintage to vintage, your best choice is to go by a wine's characteristics.

White Wines at a Glance

Wine	Characteristics
Albariño	dry
Chablis	dry, floral
Chardonnay	full, creamy
Chenin Blanc	round, creamy
Gewürztraminer	floral
Muscadet	round, dry
Pinot Blanc	round, full
Pinot Grigio	round, dry
Poilly-Fuissé	round, floral
Riesling	floral
Sauvignon Blanc	dry
Sémillon	round, full, rich
Soave	dry
Vermentino	dry
Vinho Verde	dry
Viognier	round, floral
Vouvray	round, creamy

wine vinegar   *See* vinegar.

winter melon   Although it's called a melon, winter melon has the flavor and texture of a summer squash. Substitute zucchini or yellow squash at any time, either raw or cooked in a soup.

wonton skins   *See* egg roll skins.

wood ear mushroom   *See* mushroom, dried Asian.

W

woodruff Perhaps one of the reasons why woodruff is used to flavor the famed German drink, May Wine, is that it blooms in the early spring. It has a sweet scent and herbaceous flavor. Echinacea or jasmine are good alternatives.

Worcestershire sauce Although it's based on an Indian condiment, it's named after a city in England because two chemists—Lea and Perrins—developed it there. Worcestershire sauce contains many ingredients, including garlic, soy sauce, molasses, anchovies, vinegar, and tamarind. Soy sauce, fish sauce, or steak sauce are your best options; few people want to try to make it themselves.

XXX, XXXX You'll see these symbols on boxes of confectioners' sugar. The XXXX formulation is lighter than the XXX.

Toque Tips

If you want to make whipped cream up to a few hours in advance of serving it, use confectioners' sugar rather than granulated sugar. The small amount of cornstarch it contains keeps the whipped cream stabilized and prevents it from separating.

yam   Botanically, yams and sweet potatoes are not related, but we often use the names interchangeably in this country because they're both orange-fleshed tubers that are cooked in the same way and have a similar sweet flesh. In addition to substituting one for another, you can use acorn or butternut squash as an alternative to both.

yeast   It's the yeast—microscopic, single-celled organisms—that turn starches and sugars in flour into bubbles of carbon dioxide. In eras past, yeast were collected randomly from the atmosphere, but we're luckier today; yeast is available in many easy-to-use forms.

1 (¹/₄-oz.) pkg. dry yeast = 2¹/₄ tsp. dry yeast or 1 (.6-oz.) pkg. cake dry yeast

Toque Tips

It's very important to "proof" your yeast before making a dough. By sprinkling the yeast on water that's between 105°F and 115°F and waiting for it to begin foaming, you can make sure the yeast is alive.

yellow squash   This member of the summer squash family, also called crookneck squash, has a peel that ranges from light to bright yellow. In flavor, it's almost identical to zucchini, so that's your best option; no other vegetable adds the same yellow color.

yellowfin   *See* tuna.

yellowtail   A game fish caught off the coast of California and Mexico, yellowtail is a member of the pompano family and has a texture similar to that of tuna. Tuna is a good substitution, although the flesh will be darker. Other alternatives are swordfish, grouper, or red snapper.

yogurt   If you're on a diet, there's no better friend than yogurt. It gives foods the same tangy taste of sour cream with a fraction of the calories. Yogurt is a combination of milk, low-fat milk, or skim milk into which bacteria are added to produce lactic acid, which coagulates the proteins in the milk. Greek-style yogurt is frequently made from sheep's milk rather than cow's milk, and there's also yogurt on the market now made from goat's milk. Substitute any plain nonfat yogurt for one with another fat content. Other alternatives are sour cream, crème fraîche, and silken tofu.

> **Toque Tips**
>
> It's easy to make your own fruit-flavored yogurts rather than buy-ing those that contain either refined sugar or artificial sweetener. Simply mash your favorite ripe fruit and mix in nonfat yogurt. If you want additional sweetness, add a spoonful of fruit-only jam.

yucca   This tuber is for South Americans what the potato is for Americans—the all-purpose starch that can be eaten many ways. You can look for it in Hispanic markets, or substitute a potato in recipes.

zahtar (*ZAH-tar*)   This spice blend used in Turkish cooking consists primarily of toasted sesame seeds and thyme. Combine equal portions of both for a good substitution.

zante currant   *See* raisin.

zest   The zest of citrus fruits is the colored part of the skin that contains all the aromatic oils. These oils are now available commercially, and they are an excellent substitution, although the texture of the zest won't be there.

   1 tsp. grated citrus zest = ¹/₄ tsp. citrus oil

Food Foibles

It's important when using zest that you only use the colored part of the rind. The white substance underneath, called the pith, is extremely bitter and assertive when added to food.

Zinfandel (*ZIN-fan-dell*)   *See* wine, red.

ziti (*ZEE-tee*)   *See* pasta, dried.

zucchini   Zucchini is the most popular member of the summer squash family, and because it grows prolifically in the garden, many a gardener is faced with quite a harvest each August. Yellow squash, pattypan squash, or chayote can all be used in its place.

Equipment Substitutions

Can't find your whisk? Don't have a 9×13 pan? Improvise! This appendix helps you to do that successfully.

baking pan   It's always best to use the pan specified in a recipe, but if that's not possible, you can gauge which pan to use based on capacity. Baking times and temperatures change per pan dimensions, so the best way to calculate time is to find a similar recipe specifying the size of the pan you're using.

Baking Pan Volumes

Size	Volume
$2^3/_4 \times 1^1/_2$-inch muffin	$^1/_2$ cup
8-inch round	4 cups
9-inch round	6 cups
8-inch square	6 cups
9-inch square	8 cups
9×13-inch rectangular	14 cups
$8^1/_2 \times 4^1/_2$-inch loaf	6 cups
9×5-inch loaf	8 cups

continues

Baking Pan Volumes   (continued)

Size	Volume
10×3-inch springform	12 cups
10×3$^1/_2$-inch Bundt	12 cups

baster   If you don't have a baster, make a mop out of strips of rag or paper towels; secure the mop to the handle of a wooden spoon with a rubber band. Or if the basting liquid is thin, you can use a spray bottle.

biscuit cutter   Use a juice can with both the top and bottom removed. Or try a small glass—plastic is best because the lip is frequently sharper.

blender   A food processor easily replaces a blender, as does a handheld immersion blender. Or try a food mill or ricer.

Bundt pan   Any tube pan can be used in the same way.

cake tester   The probe of an instant-read thermometer, a strand of pasta, or a bamboo skewer serve as a suitable replacement.

cheesecloth   To contain seasonings to be removed from a soup or stew, place the herbs and spices in a tea infuser or wrap them in a paper coffee filter and tie it closed with a piece of kitchen string. To strain foods, use a paper coffee filter, cotton dishtowel, or a few layers of paper towel. To form sausages to poach in hot liquid, use aluminum foil or parchment paper.

coffee filter   Try a good-quality paper napkin or doubled paper towel instead.

coffee grinder   Use your blender set on medium speed.

colander   For a small amount of food, a steamer basket can serve as a colander; for a larger quantity, use a salad spinner insert.

cookie sheet   Cover cooling racks or broiler pans with aluminum foil and place the cookies on that, or turn over a large roasting pan and bake the cookies on the bottom.

cooling rack   Use an oven shelf or a broiling pan; or for a large quantity of cookies, use a clean household window screen suspended over some pans. When the cookies are somewhat cool but still not ready for storage, transfer them to a tablecloth or a few layers of towels; the towels are porous and allow the cookies to cool well. To cool a pie, space out some table knives, alternating the direction of the handles, and place the hot pie plate on top.

custard cup   *See* ramekins.

double boiler   Improvise a double boiler by inserting a glass or stainless-steel mixing bowl in a saucepan of water. Be sure the bowl doesn't touch the water below, and hold on to the bowl with a pot holder as you whisk or stir.

dry measuring cups   Improvise with yogurt containers. A 4-ounce size is $^1/_2$ cup, an 8-ounce size is 1 cup, etc.

egg beater   A whisk does the job of an egg beater very effectively, or you can hold three table forks with their tines facing each other and secure the handles with a rubber band. Or use a pastry blender, beating with it in a circular motion.

fondue pot   When you need a fondue pot to use as a serving bowl for cheese or dessert fondues, use a slow cooker. When the pot is being used as a cooking appliance for broth or oil fondues, use a chafing dish or an electric fryer.

food processor   Use a blender to purée foods. To grate foods, use the appropriate side of a grater.

funnel   Craft a funnel from aluminum foil, wax paper, or parchment paper. Roll the paper into a cone shape, and insert it into the bottle being filled. Hold it closed carefully with one hand while pouring with the other.

grater   For coarse to fine grating, use a food processor fitted with the steel blade, pulsing on and off until the food is grated as finely as you'd like it. To create slices as you would from the slits on a box grater, use a knife or a food processor fitted with a slicing blade.

kitchen twine   Doubled or tripled dental floss holds food together nicely.

knife sharpener   The rough ring that wasn't glazed on the bottom of earthenware pottery makes a great knife sharpener. Hold the knife blade at an angle as you would if using a sharpening steel.

liquid measuring cup   A liquid measuring cup is a minimum of 1 cup (8 ounces), and it's important to use an accurate amount, especially for baking. An ice cube tray usually holds 2 tablespoons per cube, or 1 ounce. (Before baking, measure your ice cube tray to be sure it's 2 tablespoons.)

loaf pan   If you only have one loaf pan and want to bake two loaves of bread, place the pan in the center of a 9×13-inch pan, and place the bread dough on either side of it. For a quick bread dough, line the indentations with aluminum foil and grease the foil.

measuring spoons   The plastic cap of any soda bottle is exactly 1 teaspoon, and the small ridges on the inside are a measure for $1/2$ teaspoon. Three teaspoons make one tablespoon, so use the bottle cap as a guide.

meat mallet   To flatten food, use the bottom of a small, heavy saucepan or skillet; a rolling pin works, too. Hold it by the sides rather than the handle to exert even pressure on the food to be pounded. To tenderize, run a pizza cutter over the food or prick it many times with the tip of a paring knife or a meat fork.

muffin tin   Place paper liners into or grease ramekins and get the same results.

pan lid   Use a sheet of aluminum foil or any heat-proof plate. If you want to see what's cooking, use a glass pie plate.

pastry bag   Use a heavy resealable plastic bag, and push the mixture down to one corner, pressing out the air around it. Trim off the corner of the bag with scissors; the smaller the cut, the thinner the line will be, so start small and then increase the size as needed. For small amounts, make a cone from parchment paper and fill it. Then just cut off the tip and start piping.

pastry blender   Use two knives, your fingertips, or a food processor's on-and-off pulsing action.

pastry brush   Use a spray bottle for melted butter or oil. Use any inexpensive and clean paint brush, including the foam ones. Make a "mop" out of many strands of paper towels, and secure the mop to the handle of a wooden spoon with rubber bands.

peppermill   Use a coffee grinder—just be sure you wash it out well before using it for coffee beans! Or for a larger grind, place the peppercorns in a heavy plastic bag and crush them with a rolling pin or the bottom of a heavy skillet.

pie weight   Press a sheet of aluminum foil into the bottom and up the sides of the shell, and fill it with rice, dried beans, or pennies.

plastic wrap   To cover food for storage, use aluminum foil. To cook food in a microwave oven, cut open a heavy plastic bag and turn it into a sheet of plastic wrap, wrapping it around the sides of the bowl.

pot holder   To remove lightweight pans from the oven, use tongs to protect your hands or use folded dish towels or heavy winter mittens. If the hot object is a ringed pot lid, try inserting a wine cork in the handle and pick up the lid by the cork.

potato masher   Use a heavy whisk or a heavy meat fork. (Avoid using an electric appliance or your mashed potatoes may become gluey potatoes.)

ramekin (or custard cup)   Muffin tins can serve the same function; fill the unused tins with water before baking to keep the food in the adjacent tins from burning.

rice cooker   Use a slow cooker.

roasting pan   Create an impromptu pan from three or four layers of heavy-duty aluminum foil—be sure to pinch the edges closed tightly! Then set your "pan" on a baking sheet, and you're ready to roast.

rolling pin   Cover a glass bottle with a sheet of aluminum foil.

rubber scraper   Use a slotted spatula covered with aluminum foil.

ruler   Each bill of American currency is 6 inches long. I'm not advocating cutting up a dollar to gauge the size of a cube of chicken, but you can use it as a guide.

sifter   Use a wire mesh strainer and shake it back and forth. Or combine the dry ingredients in a jar with a tight-fitting lid and shake well.

soufflé dish   Any saucepan of the right volume can be used instead.

spatula   Try clean painter's putty knives in various sizes.

springform pan   Use any cake pan lined with a double layer of heavy-duty aluminum foil instead. When the cake is cool, just pull out the foil.

steamer   Any size metal colander or wire mesh strainer does the job. Just be sure the pot can still be securely closed so the steam doesn't escape.

toaster   Preheat the oven boiler, and broil food to be toasted on a baking sheet. Check often because breads can go from toasted to burnt very quickly.

toothpick   Metal skewers or even long, thin well-washed aluminum nails hold food together. As an implement, use thin pretzel sticks so even the "fork" is edible.

vegetable brush   Try a clean loofah or other exfoliating bath glove.

vegetable peeler   To peel carrots or turnips, scrape them with a chef's knife. For heavier jobs, use a paring knife or a cheese slicer.

whisk   Use the round blades of an electric mixer. Or arrange three table forks with the tines facing each other and secure the handles with a rubber band. Or use a pastry blender, beating with it in a circular motion.

zester   Use the small holes on a box grater. Cover that side of the grater with a sheet of aluminum foil so you can pull it off and retrieve all the oils.

Common Ingredient Yields

It's frustrating that ingredients are most often sold by the pound, yet recipes list them in quantities of volume. That's when this chart comes in handy.

Weights and Measures of Common Ingredients

Food	Quantity	Yield/Volume
Almonds		
Whole	1 lb.	3 cups
Slivered	1 lb.	4 cups
Anchovies		
Tin	2 oz.	10 to 12 fillets
Paste	1.6 oz.	3 TB.
Apples	1 lb.	2½ to 3 cups sliced
Apricots		
Fresh	1 lb.	2½ to 3 cups sliced
Dried	12 oz.	2 cups
Avocado	1 lb.	1 cup mashed fruit

continues

Weights and Measures of Common Ingredients   (continued)

Food	Quantity	Yield/Volume
Bacon	1 lb.	16 to 20 slices
Bananas	1 medium	1 cup sliced; ½ cup mashed
Barley	½ lb.	1 cup
Bean sprouts	¼ lb.	1 cup
Beans		
Canned	15 oz.	1¾ cups
Dried	6½ to 8 oz.	1 cup
Beets	1 lb.	3 cups diced
Bell peppers	1 lb.	3 or 4 cups sliced
Blackberries	6 oz.	1 cup
Blueberries	1 lb.	3⅓ cups
Butter	¼ lb. (1 stick)	8 TB.
Cabbage	1 lb.	4 cups packed, shredded
Cantaloupe	2 lb.	3 cups diced
Capers	4 oz. bottle	5 TB., drained
Carrots	1 lb.	3 cups diced or sliced
Cashews	5 oz.	1 cup
Celery	3 ribs	1½ cups sliced
Cheese		
Hard	¼ lb.	1 cup grated
Soft	½ lb.	1 cup
Chicken	1 whole breast	2 cups cooked and diced
Chili sauce	12 oz. bottle	1½ cups
Chocolate		
Bulk	1 oz.	3 TB. grated
Morsels	12 oz.	2 cups
Cocoa powder	1 oz.	¼ cup
Coconut, flaked	7 oz.	2½ cups
Corn		
Fresh	2 ears	1 cup kernels
Frozen	10 oz. pkg.	1½ cups kernels
Cornmeal	6 oz.	1 cup

Food	Quantity	Yield/Volume
Cornstarch	1 oz.	3 TB.
Cream	½ pt.	1 cup; 2 cups whipped
Cucumber	½ lb.	1½ to 2 cups diced
Eggplant	1 lb.	6 cups diced
Fennel	1 lb.	2½ cups sliced
Figs, fresh	1 lb.	4 cups sliced
Flour	1 lb.	3½ cups
Garlic	1 large clove	1 tsp. minced
Ginger	1 oz.	2 TB. grated
Grapefruit	1 medium	1 cup segments; 1 cup juice
Green beans		
Fresh	1 lb.	4 cups 1-in. pieces
Frozen	10 oz. pkg.	3 cups
Ham	1 lb.	3 cups diced
Hazelnuts	4¾ oz.	1 cup
Honey	1 lb.	1⅓ cups
Jam or jelly	18 oz. jar	1⅔ cups
Ketchup	1 lb.	1¾ cups
Leek	1 large	1 cup sliced, white part only
Lemons	1 medium	3 TB. juice; 2 tsp. zest
Lentils	½ lb.	1 cup
Limes	1 medium	2 TB. juice; 2 tsp. zest
Mango	1 medium	¾ cup chopped
Mayonnaise	½ lb.	1 cup
Meat, ground	1 lb.	2 cups uncooked
Milk	1 qt.	4 cups
Molasses	12 oz.	1½ cups
Mushrooms	1 lb.	5 cups sliced
Mustard	½ lb.	1 cup
Oats	¼ lb.	1 cup
Onions	1 medium	½ cup chopped

continues

Weights and Measures of Common Ingredients   (continued)

Food	Quantity	Yield/Volume
Oranges	1 medium	½ cup juice
Parsley	1 oz.	¾ cup chopped
Peaches	1 lb.	2 cups sliced
Peanut butter	18 oz. jar	2 cups
Peanuts	5 oz.	1 cup
Peas		
Fresh	1 lb.	1 cup shelled
Frozen	10 oz. pkg.	2 cups
Pecans	3½ oz.	1 cup
Peppercorns	1 oz.	3 TB.
Pine nuts	5 oz.	1 cup
Pineapple	1 medium	3 cups diced
Potato chips	4 oz. bag	2 cups crushed
Potatoes	1 lb.	3 cups sliced
Prunes	12 oz.	2 cups chopped
Pumpkin		
Canned	15 oz.	2 cups
Fresh	1 lb.	1 cup mashed
Raisins	1 lb.	3 cups
Raspberries	6 oz.	1 cup
Rice	1 lb.	2½ cups
Salt	1 oz.	1½ TB.
Scallion	1 medium	3 TB. sliced, white and green tops
Shallot	1 medium	3 TB. diced
Spinach		
Fresh	1 lb.	¾ cup cooked
Frozen	10 oz. pkg.	1¼ cups
Split peas	½ lb.	1 cup
Squash		
Summer	1 lb.	3½ cups sliced
Winter	1 lb.	2 cups chopped
Strawberries	1 pt.	1½ cups sliced

Food	Quantity	Yield/Volume
Sugar		
Brown	1 lb.	2¼ cups packed
Confectioners'	1 lb.	4 cups (unsifted)
Granulated	1 lb.	2¼ cups
Tomatoes		
Canned	14.5 oz.	1 cup drained and chopped
Cherry	1 pt.	2 cups
Fresh	1 lb.	1½ cups pulp
Paste	6 oz.	12 TB.
Sun-dried	1 oz.	3 or 4 TB. chopped
Turkey	1 lb. cooked	3 cups diced
Walnuts	4 oz.	1 cup

Metric Conversion Tables

The scientifically precise calculations needed for baking aren't necessary when cooking conventionally. The tables in this appendix are designed for general cooking, so if you're making conversions for baking, grab your calculator and compute the exact figure.

Converting Ounces to Grams

The numbers in the following table are approximate. To reach the exact amount of grams, multiply the number of ounces by 28.35.

Ounces	Grams	Ounces	Grams
1 oz.	30 g	9 oz.	250 g
2 oz.	60 g	10 oz.	285 g
3 oz.	85 g	11 oz.	300 g
4 oz.	115 g	12 oz.	340 g
5 oz.	140 g	13 oz.	370 g
6 oz.	180 g	15 oz.	425 g
7 oz.	200 g	14 oz.	400 g
8 oz.	225 g	16 oz.	450 g

Converting Quarts to Liters

The numbers in the following table are approximate. To reach the exact amount of liters, multiply the number of quarts by 0.95.

Quarts	Liters	Quarts	Liters
¼ qt. (1 cup)	¼ L	4 qt.	3¾ L
½ qt. (1 pt.)	½ L	5 qt.	4¾ L
1 qt.	1 L	6 qt.	5½ L
2 qt.	2 L	7 qt.	6½ L
2½ qt.	2½ L	8 qt.	7½ L
3 qt.	2¾ L		

Converting Pounds to Grams and Kilograms

The numbers in the following table are approximate. To reach the exact amount of grams, multiply the number of pounds by 453.6.

Pounds	Grams; Kilograms	Pounds	Grams; Kilograms
1 lb.	450 g	5 lb.	2¼ kg
1½ lb.	675 g	5½ lb.	2½ kg
2 lb.	900 g	6 lb.	2¾ kg
2½ lb.	1,125 g; 1¼ kg	6½ lb.	3 kg
3 lb.	1,350 g	7 lb.	3¼ kg
3½ lb.	1,500 g; 1½ kg	7½ lb.	3½ kg
4 lb.	1,800 g	8 lb.	3¾ kg
4½ lb.	2 kg		

Converting Fahrenheit to Celsius

The numbers in the following table are approximate. To reach the exact temperature, subtract 32 from the Fahrenheit reading, multiply the number by 5, and divide by 9.

Degrees Fahrenheit	Degrees Celsius	Degrees Fahrenheit	Degrees Celsius
170°F	77°C	350°F	180°C
180°F	82°C	375°F	190°C
190°F	88°C	400°F	205°C
200°F	95°C	425°F	220°C
225°F	110°C	450°F	230°C
250°F	120°C	475°F	245°C
300°F	150°C	500°F	260°C
325°F	165°C		

Converting Inches to Centimeters

The numbers in the following table are approximate. To reach the exact number of centimeters, multiply the number of inches by 2.54.

Inches	Centimeters	Inches	Centimeters
½ in.	1.5 cm	7 in.	18 cm
1 in.	2.5 cm	8 in.	20 cm
2 in.	5 cm	9 in.	23 cm
3 in.	8 cm	10 in.	25 cm
4 in.	10 cm	11 in.	28 cm
5 in.	13 cm	12 in.	30 cm
6 in.	15 cm		

Quick Reference Charts

You'll find the weight and volume of hundreds of ingredients listed in their alphabetical entries in this book. These charts give you common measurements you might confront every day—all at a glance.

Liquid Measures

When either multiplying or dividing recipes, it's useful to have these measurements handy. Keep in mind that amounts up to 1 tablespoon are measured in spoons of graduated sizes, and liquids should always be poured into a liquid measuring cup, not in a graduated dry cup:

3 teaspoons = 1 tablespoon

2 tablespoons = 1 ounce

1 jigger = 3 tablespoons = 1½ ounces

4 tablespoons = ¼ cup

6 tablespoons = ⅓ cup

8 tablespoons = ½ cup

10 tablespoons = ⅔ cup

12 tablespoons = ¾ cup

16 tablespoons = 1 cup

2 cups = 1 pint = ½ quart

1 pint = 1 pound liquid weight

2 pints = 1 quart

2 quarts = ½ gallon

4 quarts = 1 gallon

Dry Measures

While almost all liquids weigh the same amount, the same cannot be said for dry ingredients. Their weight depends on the density of ingredients, but still, certain measures remain standard. The measuring spoons are the same for dry and liquid ingredients; the cups for dry ingredients come in graduated sizes from ¼ cup to 1 cup.

½ cup = 2 × ¼ cup measures

⅔ cup = 2 × ⅓ cup measures

1 cup = 4 × ¼ cup measures = 3 × ⅓ cup measures = 2 × ½ cup measures

Common Ingredient Measures

The density of ingredients determines their weight in relation to their volume. Here are some you encounter frequently:

1 tablespoon butter = ⅛ stick = ½ ounce

8 tablespoons butter = 1 stick = 4 ounces = ¼ pound

4 sticks butter = 1 pound

1 tablespoon unsifted flour = ¼ ounce

½ cup unsifted flour = 2½ ounces

1 cup unsifted flour = 5 ounces

1 pound unsifted flour = 3½ cups

Note: 1 cup sifted flour = 1 cup unsifted flour – 1½ tablespoons

1 tablespoon granulated sugar = ½ ounce

½ cup granulated sugar = 3½ ounces

1 cup granulated sugar = 7 ounces

1 pound granulated sugar = 2⅓ cups

About the Author

For the past 30 years, **Ellen Brown** has spent her life as the consummate "foodie," following a career path that encompasses both writing and hands-on cooking.

Ellen gained the national limelight in 1982 as the founding food editor of *USA Today*. She was previously senior feature writer for *The Cincinnati Enquirer*, where her areas of coverage included restaurants, food, art, interior design, and fashion.

Ellen has written a shelf of cookbooks since leaving *USA Today* in 1986. The most recent additions are *The Complete Idiot's Guide to Cooking with Mixes* (2004), *The Complete Idiot's Guide to Smoothies* (2005), *The Complete Idiot's Guide to Cover and Bake Meals* (2005), *The Complete Idiot's Guide to Fondues and Hot Dips* (2006), *The Complete Idiot's Guide to Juicing* (2007), *The Complete Idiot's Guide to Cooking for Two* (2007), *The Complete Idiot's Guide to Fast and Fresh Meals* (2007), and *The Complete Idiot's Guide to Slow Cooker Cooking, Second Edition* (2007), all published by Alpha Books.

The *Nantucket Cuisine* cookbook, based on recipes developed for the catering business she ran in Nantucket for 4 years, was published in 2002. It was preceded by *All Wrapped Up* in 1998, which was one of the first books to bring new, contemporary wrapped foods into the home kitchen. Ellen is also the author of the IACP/Seagrams Award–winning *Gourmet Gazelle Cookbook*, Tastemaker Award–winning *Cooking with the New American Chefs*, *The Great Chefs of Chicago*, *Southwest Tastes*, and *Great Chefs of the East*.

Ellen's writing has appeared in more than two dozen publications, including *The Washington Post*, the *Los Angeles Times* syndicate, the Prodigy computer network, *Bon Appétit*, *Art Culinaire*, *Museum and Arts Washington*, *Texas Monthly*, *The Baltimore Sun*, *The San Francisco Chronicle*, *Ft. Lauderdale News Sentinel*, *Tables*, *Good Food*, *Dossier*, *Showcase*, and *Diversion*.

In 1985, Ellen was honored by *Cook's Magazine*, who selected her for inclusion in the prestigious "Who's Who of Cooking in America." Profiles of her have appeared in *The Washington Post*, *The Detroit News*, *Coastal Living*, *The Miami Herald*, and on TV's Food Network. She is a member of the International Association of Culinary Professionals, the James Beard Foundation, and the Commanderie de Bordeaux.

Ellen lives in Providence, Rhode Island, with Tigger-Cat Brown and Patches-Kitten Brown, her cats, who personally endorse all the fish and seafood substitutions in this book.